THE TOMB OF TUT·ANKH·AMEN

A CARVED IVORY PANEL

The scene represents Tut·ankh·Amen and his Queen Ankh·es·en·Amen in a pavilion.
From a lid of a box.

(*See* p. 118)

THE TOMB OF TUT·ANKH·AMEN

DISCOVERED BY THE LATE EARL OF CARNARVON AND HOWARD CARTER

By

HOWARD CARTER

Hon. Sc.D. (Yale University) ; Correspondent
Real Academia de la Historia, Madrid

With Appendices by

DOUGLAS E. DERRY, M.B., Ch.B. : A. LUCAS,
O.B.E., F.I.C.

The Annexe and Treasury

With 156 Illustrations from Photographs by
HARRY BURTON
(Of the Metropolitan Museum of Art, New York)

Duckworth

First published in 1933 by Cassell & Company Ltd
Reprinted in 2000 by permission of
The Griffith Institute, Oxford

Gerald Duckworth & Co. Ltd.
61 Frith Street, London W1V 5TA
Tel: 0207 434 4242
Fax: 0207 434 4420
Email: enquiries@duckworth-publishers.co.uk
www.ducknet.co.uk

A catalogue record for this book is available
from the British Library

ISBN 0 7156 2964 6

Printed in Great Britain by Bath Press, Bath

FOREWORD

'At first I could see nothing, the hot air escaping from the chamber causing the candle flame to flicker, but presently, as my eyes grew accustomed to the light, details of the room within emerged slowly from the mist, strange animals, statues, and gold – everywhere the glint of gold. For the moment – an eternity it must have seemed to the others standing by – I was struck dumb with amazement, and when Lord Carnarvon, unable to stand the suspense any longer, inquired anxiously, "Can you see anything?" it was all I could do to get out the words, "Yes, wonderful things" ...'

(Howard Carter and Arthur C. Mace, *The Tomb of Tut.ankh.Amen. Search, Discovery and the Clearance of the Antechamber*, pp. 95-6)

On 4 November, 1922, Howard Carter and his sponsor, the fifth Earl of Carnarvon, made a discovery in Egypt's Valley of the Kings which would change the face of archaeology for good. For the first time in recorded history, diggers had stumbled upon the virtually intact burial of an Egyptian pharaoh – the boy-king Tutankhamun, son and successor of the heretic Akhenaten; and it was a tomb piled high with funerary treasures and gold. The popular perception of Egyptology changed overnight: no longer the worthy pursuit of dusty academics, it was now seen as high-stakes adventure. Without the excitement engendered by

Tutankhamun, it is doubtful that Indiana Jones would ever have been born.

The story of the find reads like a fairytale fiction: how Carter dug for years with little success in pursuit of the impossible dream; how, in his final season, the tomb he sought was found; how this tomb impacted upon the world, turning its discoverers into celebrities overnight; and how, with the unexpected death of Lord Carnarvon (supposed victim of 'the pharaoh's curse'), the triumph turned sour.

The careful documentation and clearance of Tutankhamun's tomb, and the transportation to Cairo of the objects interred there, took Howard Carter the best part of a decade, with the excavator's personal narrative of the work appearing in three wonderfully written, self-contained volumes published between 1923 and 1933. This, the third in the trilogy, describes the excavation of two of the store chambers – the Treasury and the Annexe – within which had been gathered many of the boy-king's most precious funerary treasures. Published in a relatively small edition in 1933, the book soon went out of print and has for many years been virtually unobtainable.

For all his riches, Tutankhamun was in life a relatively insignificant king, too young to impose his personality on the state he ruled and intentionally forgotten by those who came after. With the discovery of his tomb, his name was at long last 'made to live': today, more than three thousand years after his death, Egypt's boy-king stands as a veritable icon not only of Egyptology itself, but of archaeological endeavour as a whole.

London, January 2000   Nicholas Reeves

PREFACE

THIS volume deals with the two small store chambers of the tomb : the one adjoining the Burial Chamber, the other adjoining the Antechamber. They were originally called the Store Chamber and Annexe, but I have re-named them the Innermost Treasury and Store-room. As a matter of fact the ancient Egyptians called these small chambers " Treasuries," and they were known as the " Right " or " Left-hand Treasury," or " Treasury of the Innermost," in accordance with their situation and purpose. As the room called the " Treasury of the Innermost " seems to have been the storehouse for the Canopic equipment and other chattels, I have named the corresponding room in this tomb the Innermost Treasury.

If one compares the plan of this tomb with a normal Eighteenth Dynasty royal hypogeum, that of Thothmes IV being perhaps the best example, one immediately sees that this tomb is a modification of the Sepulchral Hall and " Well " (i.e. the sunken space at the end of the hall for the sarcophagus) without any of the corridors and chambers that should lead to it. Thus, the room called the Antechamber here is a modified form of the Sepulchral Hall, the Burial Chamber the " Well," and the Innermost Treasury and Annexe are but two of the four storehouses or treasuries that belong to the normal Sepulchral Hall and " Well " for the sarcophagus.

Preface

This volume also closes the preliminary narrative of the discovery and contents of the Tomb of Tut·ankh·Amen. A summary of the ten seasons' work spent upon preserving, recording, and transporting the whole of the material to the Cairo Museum. The second season was spent alone upon dismantling those four great sepulchral shrines that shielded the sarcophagus, and the last two seasons upon consolidating them fit for transport. They, with the rest of the tomb furniture, are now safely housed and exhibited in that museum.

Since the understanding that was reached with the Ziwar Government, in 1925, with regard to recognition for the discovery, the work and heavy expenses borne by the Carnarvon estate, and the benefits resulting to Egypt generally, Egypt has experienced five successive governments. In 1930, the Wafdists Cabinet, under the premiership of H.E. Nahas Pasha, decided not to allow any of the antiquities belonging to the discovery to leave the country and, in place of the duplicates that were promised, to grant a monetary recompense.

It is for that reason that I think it only fair to make the following statement : The brunt of practically the whole of the work was borne by the Carnarvon estate and Almina, Countess of Carnarvon. It was assisted by the courtesy of the Trustees and Director of the Metropolitan Museum of Art, New York, who generously lent the valuable services of Mr. Arthur Mace, Mr. Harry Burton, and Messrs. Hauser and Hall. And, by the courtesy of the Egyptian Government, I received each winter the good assistance of Mr. A. Lucas, the Government Chemist, attached to the Cairo Museum. The cost of the preliminary excavations and the work done in dealing with the contents of the tomb, borne by the Carnarvon estate and Almina, Countess of Carnarvon, amounted to £36,000, and the labour lent by the Metropolitan Museum of Art was estimated at £8,000, thus making a total cost of £44,000 sterling. During the autumn of 1930, the Egyptian Government paid to the Carnarvon estate and Almina, Countess of Carnarvon, a sum equivalent to £36,000 sterling.

The cost of consolidating the four great shrines for transport to Cairo, which occupied the last two seasons, ending in February, 1932, was covered by the Egyptian Government and myself.

The funerary equipment of an ancient Egyptian tomb is a fertile subject for study. It abounds with material of former times, and of the tastes, the manners and customs of successive generations. Its furniture, clothing and ornaments, its implements of war and of the chase, its very walking-sticks and staves, all furnish food for thought and interesting speculation. Among purely ritualistic paraphernalia belonging to a burial custom one finds simple family relics which must have carried many a human remembrance. By their study we are able to picture in our minds the habits and character of a people to whom they belonged. And in that pursuit, should we find an object that appears to us as merely curious, or perhaps even repellent, it must be remembered that with a religion long forgotten, an object pertaining to its ritual, an image of its god, ceases to be felt as any more than a human device—its religious power has gone.

From this burial we glean an interesting fact which may possibly throw not a little light upon the history of the Egyptian monarchs of dynastic times. The heirs were associated with the throne when they were quite young. Apparently to ensure the dynasty they were married as early as it was possible, and thus made partners of the sovereign. In the case of Tut·ankh·Amen and the hereditary princess Ankh·es·en·Amen, they were associated with the throne when they were but nine and ten years of age. And I would here remark that throughout Egyptian dynastic history, whenever we have evidence of the probable age of a king at the time of his death, and the length of his reign, we find that he must have ascended the throne during his early youth, in some cases when still an infant.

Since writing the introduction to this volume I learn that a record giving a regnal year XIX of Akh·en·Aten has been discovered recently at El Amarna by the officers of the Egypt Exploration Society. This shows that the king lived at least two years longer than has hitherto been suspected. It is difficult, however, to imagine that the chronologers for the government under Rameses II, hardly a century later, were unaware of the length of Akh·en·Aten's reign as well as the reigns of his immediate successors, when they attributed the fifty-nine years to Hor·em·heb (p. 28). An explanation may possibly be that the co-regencies overlapped even longer than suspected. Wine-jars in this tomb (p. 147) show that the Aten Domain was maintained at least twenty-one years. The study of that period presents many difficulties ; data, and the strictest investigation is still much in need.

To the numerous colleagues who have been so good as to help whenever called upon, I would here tender

Preface

my grateful thanks, especially to Dr. Alan Gardiner
for his kind aid in translating the inscriptions.
Through the generosity of the Trustees and Director
of the Metropolitan Museum of Art I have had the
advantage of Mr. Harry Burton's unremitting labours,
to them, and to him, I owe a debt of gratitude.

HOWARD CARTER.

LUXOR, *November, 1932.*

CONTENTS

LIST OF PLATES

List of Plates

List of Plates

List of Plates

INTRODUCTION

FACTS AND THEORIES RELATING TO THE KINGS INVOLVED IN THE ATEN HERESY

IN the endeavour to obtain a correct perspective view of the kings involved in the Aten heresy, namely, Amen·hetep III, Amen·hetep IV (Akh·en·Aten), Smenkh·ka·Re, Tut·ankh·Aten (Tut·ankh·Amen), and the Divine father King Ay, one is perplexed by many difficulties and perforce by the lack of sufficient data. Of their true histories we have but little which is trustworthy, and considering how numerous are their monuments it is astonishing how disproportionate the data gleaned from them. The few historical documents that we have are of a very miscellaneous character. An occasional weather-beaten inscription upon a cliff face, a scarab, or a piece of linen, a scrap of papyrus, or a potsherd, which chance has preserved and brought to light. Hints from the numerous reliefs and paintings in the temples and tomb chapels of this age are the only other source of our knowledge upon the subject. And they (chiefly in extensive inscriptions) consist, for the most part, of conventional phrases in laudation of the king, either as a mighty ruler, a mighty pillar of the religion, or as the sole earthly representative and mouthpiece of the supreme god. From them it is but in isolated instances that we are able to gather some knowledge of those kings and their households; with the result that numbers of important questions and details remain unanswered, save from our own conjectural resources.

Searching those records, it is only here and there that the veil which shrouds those monarchs seems for an instant to be lifted, and we catch a glimpse of some amazing or puzzling fact. The domestic side of their lives and deeds in many ways can only be surmised, and, from such material as we have, we can only form our conclusions by a process of deduction.

Another source of trouble is the ambiguity of the dates upon their monuments; these in themselves are anachronistic, for they combine both the regnal and the civil year. Hence, unless we are aware of the exact civil year, month and day of a king's accession, those dates are nearly useless for any exact computation of time. For example, year 1, month 3, of the third season, of such and such a reign, might represent one year and eleven months, or only thirteen months, from the date of the king's accession. When necessary, to overcome this difficulty, and to arrive at a mean, equally removed from the two extremes, I have reckoned the seasons, months and days quoted on the monuments from the civil year as half a regnal year.

I make this plaint, not to depreciate the value of those ancient monuments and records, nor to disparage the student, but merely as a brief for the "may-bes" and "probables" in the following—what must necessarily be—tentative chronology of the sequence of events.

Manetho in Josephus states that Amen·hetep III reigned thirty years and ten months, yet there are monuments of his dated as late as the xxxvɪɪth regnal year, and if we accept a lintel scene in the tomb of Huya, mentioned below, showing an equipoise of two royal households (i.e. of Amen·hetep ɪɪɪ and ɪv), his reign must have extended to about his xʟth regnal year.

This discrepancy may be accounted for in a graffito upon the pyramid temple of Medum, written in ink from the ever-ready Egyptian palette of " the scribe May," who went " to see the very great pyramid of Horus-the-Soul of King Se·neferu." The graffito reads : " *Year xxx, under the majesty of the King Neb·maat·Re, Son of Amen, resting in truth, Amen· hetep (ɪɪɪrd), prince of Thebes, lord of might, prince of joy, who loves him that hates injustice of heart, placing the male offspring upon the seat of his father, and establishing his inheritance in the land.*" The " heir " referred to in this graffito can be no less than Amen· hetep ɪv, who afterwards assumed the name Akh·en· Aten. There was probably some reason for establishing this young prince upon the throne, and the difference, such as we find between Manetho's statement and the Egyptian monuments, is due to a co-regency between those two kings. The thirty years and ten months ascribed to Amen·hetep ɪɪɪ by Manetho is evidently the length of his reign as sole king.

The principal dated monuments prior to this co-regency are : (1) a scarab recording the king's marriage to Tyi, the daughter of Yua and Thua, which must have taken place before his ɪɪnd regnal year (*see* next scarab). Most probably at the time of his accession when he was about nine years of age ; (2) inscriptions in Turra and El-Bersheh quarries which were opened in his iiird regnal year; (3) a scarab of the iiird year recording a wild cattle hunt, wherein the Great-King's-Wife Tyi is mentioned; (4) two stelæ at the first cataract recording a Nubian campaign in his vith regnal year; (5) a scarab recording 102 lions killed by His Majesty between his ist and xth regnal years; (6) a scarab dated " year x," recording his marriage to a foreign princess Kirgipa, the daughter of Satirna, King of Naharin; (7) a scarab recording the construction of a pleasure lake in his xiith regnal year; and (8) his first jubilee celebration, between his xxxth and xxxist regnal years, recorded in the tomb of the Vizier Kha·em·hat at Thebes.

Subsequent to his co-regency with his son, Amen·hetep iv, we find the following dated monuments: a mortuary temple edict, which legally established in perpetuity an endowment for the maintenance of the king's mortuary cult, publicly read in his mortuary temple at Thebes, is dated in the year xxxiind of Amen·hetep iii's reign; upon an altar at Gebel Silsileh year xxxv is mentioned; his third jubilee celebration is recorded in the tomb of a certain Kheruf, under the following heading: " *Year xxxvi. Conducting the companions for presentation in the (royal) presence at the third jubilee of His Majesty.*" Mentioning Queen Tyi in the titulary; and a stela of similar date at Sarbut-el-Khadem in Sinai records an expedition thither in that year. Mr. Winlock discovered a date of this reign as late as the xxxviith year, in the king's palace at Thebes, south of Medinet Habou. There being no indication in those records of the existence of a co-regency, let us turn from the inscriptional to the more plastic material.

4

Introduction

A unique scene upon a lintel in the tomb of Huya, at El Amarna, furnishes us with juxtaposed pictures of the two royal households, namely, those of Amen·hetep III and Akh·en·Aten. This equipoise of the two households not only confirms the co-regency of the two kings, but gives reason to suppose that Amen·hetep III continued to live for at least a year or so after the birth of Akh·en·Aten's fourth daughter, Nefer·nefru·Aten·ta·sheri. Below this scene the prayer of Huya on the left door-jamb repeats the familiar salutation of the three worshipful powers, the Aten, the King, and the Queen, but the powers saluted on the right jamb are Akh·en·Aten, his father Amen·hetep III, and his mother Tyi. The illustration to this text is furnished by the lintel scene above. The picture is divided into two halves, that on the left showing the household of Akh·en·Aten ; that on the right the household of Amen·hetep III. In the former scene, Akh·en·Aten and his Queen Nefer·titi are represented seated, side by side, on a couch, and facing them are their four daughters waving fans. The counter-picture shows Amen·hetep III in a close-fitting *nems*-cap, sitting on a chair, as if in the act of addressing his wife, who occupies a seat facing him, with the Princess Bakt·Aten at her knee. Represented above both households is the Aten disk, and rays offering the symbol of life impartially. The picture at least intensifies known or suspected facts; and we glean from it that Amen·hetep III must have been living at least a year or so after the birth of Akh·en·Aten's fourth daughter, namely, about his xlth regnal year, when he had reached at least forty-nine years of age, coinciding probably with Akh·en·Aten's ixth regnal year. Judging from the stature of Bakt·Aten, figured in this picture, she was about the same age as Ankh·es·en·pa·Aten.

The extraordinary similarity of the figure of Amen·hetep III, in the right-hand scene just mentioned, to a seated king represented on a small unfinished stela in the Berlin Museum (No. 20,716), found at El Amarna, leads one to believe that both works were by the same artist, and, one is tempted to say, possibly by the sculptor, Auta, who is figured in Huya's tomb completing a statuette of Bakt·Aten. On the Berlin stela two kings under the disk and rays of Aten are indubitably represented. Akh·en·Aten is probably the king standing on the right; he wears the *khepres*-crown, and pours wine into the cup of the king on the left, who is seated and attired in precisely the same manner as Amen·hetep III in the lintel scene. This stela seems to be another echo of the two kings associated in a co-regency, in which Akh·en·Aten, without doubt, became the supreme monarch.

Queen Tyi, the mother of Amen·hetep IV, was not of royal birth; she was the daughter of a court official and his wife, who are known to us as Yua and Thua. Hence Tyi's exalted titles, " Hereditary Princess, Mistress of the North and South, The-King's-Great-Wife, Lady of the Two Lands," were not hereditary, but were attained through her marriage to Amen·hetep III. She was the official, the favourite, and the principal wife of the king, and for that reason her father, Yua, reached high rank, and, possibly by his being the parent of the queen, he was designated " Divine Father." Thus Amen·hetep IV could not be claimed to be wholly royal, and that may be part reason for " placing the male offspring upon the seat of his father, and establishing his inheritance in the Land " noticed in the last phrases of that Medum graffito previously mentioned.

Amen·hetep III seems also not to have been of entirely royal blood, inasmuch as special scenes and inscriptions in the temple of Amen at Luxor, like those made for Queen Hat·shep·sût at Deir-el-Bahari, give him a supernatural birth and coronation by the gods ; in other words proclaiming his birth to have been no less than divine. Later, in various proclamations, his son, Amen·hetep IV, appears as the son of " The Father Aten," a divinity given both godly epithets and kingly titulary.

Be that as it may, his inheritance was established, he was placed upon the seat of his father, and he became virtually dictator. Within seven years of this co-regency Aten became the supreme divinity and supreme over-lord. This Aten, who thus replaced Amen, was entitled " The Father," and was considered as having commenced his reign as a supreme god and over-king on the same day as his future prophet and restorer, Amen·hetep IV.

The Aten had long been known, but Amen·hetep IV seems to have been the medium through whom his real nature and supreme dignity was discovered.

Battiscombe Gunn rightly points out that the chief purpose of naming that god : " Re lives, Harakhte, who rejoices on the Horizon in his name : ' Shu who is Aten,' " was to establish the equation Aten = Harakhte = Re, and thus proclaim the identity of Aten with other purely solar gods of Egypt from the beginning of history, and so consolidate and legitimize his position as the supreme god. Atenism, so far from attempting an entire break with the past, was a direct bid for the adherence of the older solar cults. And one wonders whether this movement was not the result of contendings for supremacy between the North and South—between the partisans of Re-Harakhte of Heliopolis, and the partisans of Amen of Thebes. However, one point is clear, the supremacy of Aten waxed and waned with the reign of Akh·en·Aten.

Within seven years, dating from Amen·hetep IV's accession, a city was founded ostensibly for " his father Aten," 250 miles north of Thebes and 200 miles south of Heliopolis, as the river flows, whither Akh·en·Aten's court was removed. Boundary tablets were erected demarcating this site, generally called El Amarna, but which is more properly known by its name Akh·et·Aten. Upon those tablets we read that before the companions of the king, the great and mighty ones, the captains of the soldiers, etc., of the land in its entirety, His Majesty said: " *Behold Akh·et·Aten which the Aten desires me to make unto him as a monument in the great name of my Majesty for ever : it was Aten my father that brought me to Akh·et·Aten. Not a noble directed me to it, not any man in the whole land directed me to it saying ' It is fitting for His Majesty that he make an Horizon-of-Aten in this place.' Nay, but it was the Aten my father that directed me to it, to make it for him as an Horizon-of-Aten. . . . I will make Akh·et·Aten for the Aten my father in this place. I will not make for him Akh·et·Aten south of it, north of it, west of it, or east of it. I will not pass beyond the southern tablet of Akh·et·Aten southward, neither will I pass beyond the northern tablet of Akh·et·Aten northward, to make for him Akh·et·Aten therein ; neither will I make for him*

8

on the western side of Akh·et·Aten. Nay, but I will make Akh·et·Aten for the Aten my father upon the Orient side of Akh·et·Aten . . . neither shall the Queen say unto me, 'Behold there is a goodly place for Akh·et·Aten in another place' and I hearken unto her : . . .''
The king then recounts the various buildings he will make within Akh·et·Aten, and says : " *There shall be made for me a sepulchre in the Orient mountain ; my burial shall be made therein . . . and the burial of the chief wife of the king, Nefer·titi, shall be made therein . . . and the burial of the king's daughter, Mert·Aten, shall be made in it. . . . The tombs of the 'Great of Seeing,' and the divine fathers of Aten, and the priests of Aten, . . . the tombs of the officers, shall be made in the Orient mountain of Akh·et·Aten and they shall be buried therein.*''

The king's speech here brings to mind an old French saying, " *Qui s'excuse s'accuse,*'' and the impression makes this new city appear uncommonly like an asylum for the young king who, influenced by obscure powers within the royal court, became the prophet and mouthpiece of a politico-religious movement.

From that moment great activity must have followed, for the new royal residence-town speedily grew and prospered. Temples and tombs, palaces and dwellings, sprang up. The hammer took precedence of the chisel, from the southernmost to the northernmost borders of the Empire, the Amen element was hammered out and the Aten chiselled in. The old and quiescent Amen·hetep III was robbed of his nomen, and he spent the rest of his life with only his prenomen, Neb·maat·Re. The Aten, by being the god of the king's capital, became the capital god.

Introduction

In its new residence the Aten schism burst into bloom, but like most exotic growths it lasted only a short time, barely ten or eleven years.

When the reaction in favour of Amen triumphed, the city of Akh·et·Aten was destroyed, and the king's mummy, buried in the royal tomb in the Orient mountain, was transferred to a rough rock-cut cell in the Valley of the Tombs of the Kings, in order to save it from the wrath of the victorious sectarians. Judging from the seals found in that cache, it would appear that it was Tut·ankh·Amen who planned and executed its transference.[1]

The remains of Akh·en·Aten's skeleton were minutely examined by Professor Elliot Smith, who maintained that the age at death was about twenty-five or twenty-six years ; however, in response to strong pressure from archæologists, he said : " No anatomist would be justified in denying that this individual may have been twenty-eight, but it is highly improbable that he could have attained thirty years if he had been normal." Dr. Douglas Derry also examined the skeleton, and he came to the conclusion that it was of a man not more than about twenty-four years of age.

However, a sculpture from a Karnak monument, dated Year v of the king's reign, represents Akh·en·

---

[1] This cache of Akh·en·Aten, discovered in the Tombs of the Kings by Mr. Theodore M. Davis, in the year 1907, was named, for some obscure reason, " The Tomb of Queen Tîyi." However, the mummy found therein is that of a man, and the evidence points to it being that of Akh·en·Aten. Recently, Mr. Engelbach, the Curator of the Cairo Museum, based from the formulæ inscribed upon the coffin, gave reasons for believing the remains to be those of Smenkh·ka·Re, but, as Dr. Alan Gardiner has pointed out to me, those inscriptions refer to a woman and not to a man. It is well known that during those ancient transportations of the royal mummies to safer places, especially after violations had taken place, any temporary or useful coffin at hand was employed for the purpose.

Aten still bearing his original names, and shows him accompanied by two daughters, the youngest at least a year old. The king's age at that time could not therefore have been less than fifteen or sixteen, and if by adding his subsequent twelve regnal years it would be difficult to admit of his age being less than twenty-seven or twenty-eight years at the time of his death.

This estimate of the age of Akh·en·Aten cannot be far wrong, for, in the endeavour to work out the dates and events of the reign, one finds that this king was at most in his twenty-eighth year when he died, and it is even possible that he died at the age of twenty-seven. There are certainly no physical reasons for considering him to have been older, but the laws of nature make it difficult to admit of him being younger.

Now, as we have regnal dates of Akh·en·Aten —upon wine-jars discovered at El Amarna—extending up to the regnal year XVII, it is fairly clear that he was about ten years of age when he came to the throne, and as this event appears to have taken place towards the end of the XXXIst regnal year of his father, he must have been born during the XXIst regnal year of that king.

This means that Amen·hetep IV was married to the Princess Nefer·titi when he was about ten.

Who Nefer·titi really was is unknown. Neither is there anything to tell us her age, further than judging from the various scenes upon the monuments, where she appears to be about the same age as her husband. By rights she should have been the crown-princess; as it is very doubtful if a prince could reign except as the husband of the heiress of the kingdom, the right to which, in accordance with the ancient Egyptian law of succession, descended in the female line. Her parentage has been assigned to Queen Tyi, but that has been contested. According to Petrie she might possibly have been Tadukhipa, the daughter of King Dushratta of Mitanna by an Egyptian princess, and was given the name Nefer·titi when in Egypt, which was changed later to Nefer· nefru·Aten·nefer·titi. A letter in cuneiform from Dushratta shows that Amen·hetep III asked for a daughter to be Mistress of Egypt, and in another letter Dushratta calls Napkhuriria (? cuneiform for Nefer·khepru·Re, i.e. Amen·hetep IV) his son-in-law, and speaks of himself as father-in-law, so, in the face of such facts, Tadukhipa and Nefer·titi may possibly be one and the same person, but there is nothing yet to prove such a view. It would be more likely that she was the daughter of Amen·hetep III, for it was by this marriage that Prince Amen·hetep (IV) ascended the throne.

In the sequence of events that follow, an important factor which must be taken into consideration is the arrival of the age of puberty. In England, legally, pubescence is at fourteen in boys, and twelve in girls; in Egypt, according to Dr. Saleh Bey Hambdy, pubescence takes place in boys about twelve or thirteen years of age. During dynastic times possibly earlier. Thus, in the case of Amen· hetep IV, it will not be unreasonable to place this event at the age 12–13, i.e. during his IInd and IIIrd regnal years.

Our interest now centres on a group of six little girls, the progeny, or rather the outcome, of his marriage with Nefer·titi. Allowing an average period of fifteen months between the birth of each child, and pubescence having taken place between 12 and 13, Amen·hetep IV would have reached his twentieth birthday when his sixth and youngest daughter, Setep·en·Re, was born, i.e. either before or just after the completion of his xth regnal year. The eldest daughter, Mert·Aten, would thus appear to have been born towards the end of his IVth regnal year, and his second daughter, Makt·Aten, when he had completed his vth regnal year—a Karnak monument dated " year v," previously mentioned, shows two daughters. As a result of the above inference, the third princess, Ankh·es·en·pa·Aten, was born early in his VIIth regnal year—a boundary stela at El Amarna, dated " year VI " and so many months, with a subsequent date, " year VIII," shows three daughters, namely, Mert·Aten, Makt·Aten, and Ankh·es·en·pa·Aten. It should be noted, however, that the figure of Ankh·es·en·pa·Aten appears as if it might have been added after the original conception of the stela. In this way the fourth, fifth, and sixth daughters came into the world approximately as follows: Nefer·nefru·Aten·ta·sheri during the middle of the VIIIth, Nefer·nefru·Re towards the end of the IXth, and Setep·en·Re about the completion of the xth, or the beginning of the XIth regnal years.

In the tomb of Meryre (II), at El Amarna, there is a scene representing " Tribute of the South brought to the King," and it is dated " year XII " and so many months. Here the king and the queen have their six daughters standing behind them. The sixth daughter, Setep·en·Re, is depicted able to walk and play with her sister, Nefer·nefru·Re, who holds a young gazelle in her arms, which suggests the youngest daughter to have been already in her second year at that time—i.e. the king's xiith regnal year and so many months. Among many such scenes, in the El Amarna private mortuary chapels, depicting these children, the relative age of each child is shown by her height. Careful discrimination of that kind excludes the possibility of twin births, and is therefore serviceable when estimating their ages.

A reckoning such as the above cannot of course be considered exact, but the error cannot be more than say a year. The evidence of that dated scene enables us to corroborate the approximate age of the king at the time of death; viz. $12\frac{1}{2}$ years for pubescence, plus $7\frac{1}{2}$ years for the six daughters, plus 2 years for the age of the youngest daughter $=$ 22 years $=$ the xiith regnal year and so many months, plus the remaining 5 years of his reign $=$ 27 years. It therefore does not seem unreasonable to place the event " Tribute of the South " as taking place when the king was in his twenty-third year, and his death some time during his twenty-eighth year.

Although the revolutionary movement, both in religion as well as in art, is visible on Theban monuments dating from the earlier years of Amen·hetep iv, a letter written to the king, dated " year v, month 7, day 14," by a steward of his in Memphis, giving the king the following titles, " Great of Rule in Karnak, Ruler of Thebes," and referring to Ptah and other gods, makes it manifest that the king was then still in Thebes and had not yet abandoned the old religion. Moreover, wine-jar inscriptions found at El Amarna extend to year v under the name Amen· hetep (iv), and from year vi to year xvii under the name Akh·en·Aten ; and the earliest mention of the king's new name (Akh·en·Aten) seems to be on the boundary stelæ of Akh·et·Aten, dated in the year VI, month 8, day 13.

In the face of such facts, the king did not move his court to the new site until some time in his VIIth regnal year; nor did the Aten arrive at dominant control and receive his full names and titulary— "*May the Good God live, who takes pleasure in Truth, Lord of all that Aten encompasses, Lord of Heaven, Aten, the Living, the Great, who illumines the Two Lands, may the Father live : ' Re lives, Harakhte, who rejoices on the Horizon in his name :' ' Shu who is Aten,' who is given life for ever and ever, Aten, the Living, the Great, who is in Jubilee, who dwells in the Temple of Aten in Akh·et·Aten*"—before that date. It was then, by the agency of his son and prophet, he attained undisputed supremacy as king-god of the universe. And, as Gunn suggests, the king's new name, Akh·en·Aten (i.e. " It-is-well-with-Aten "), may be direct allusion to this happy restoration. It should be noted, however, that for some reason a change was made in the cartouche-names of Aten. In place of the earlier forms, quoted above, we find : "*Re lives, Ruler of the Horizon, who rejoices on the Horizon in his name : ' Re the Father, who has returned to Aten.'*" This change of name seems to mark some event, and it seems to have taken place about the VIIIth year of the reign.

Striking but pathetic pictures in the royal tomb at El Amarna show that the king's second daughter, Makt·Aten, died while still of tender age. In the scene depicting her obsequies, we see the whole royal family and household lamenting over the body of this little child. In that scene of lament, Mert·Aten,

Ankh·es·en·pa·Aten, and Nefer·nefru·Aten·ta·sheri, are represented in accordance with their relative ages, but a fourth daughter, undoubtedly Nefer·nefru·Re, is shown as a small babe in the arms of her nurse. Makt·Aten seems then to have died a short time after the birth of her sister Nefer·nefru·Re, when she was some five and a half years old, i.e. at the beginning of her father's xth regnal year.

For the date when Amen·hetep III died we have to rely on conjecture—probably his death occurred about the same time as that of Makt·Aten. A year or so after that event, we find Akh·en·Aten associated with another co-regent. The Crown-Princess Mert·Aten, who could not have been more than nine years of age, was married, possibly to avert some crisis, to a dim princeling known to us as Smenkh·ka·Re. Just when this marriage occurred is not certain, but the sequence of events that follow point to it having taken place about the xIIIth regnal year of Akh·en·Aten. We learn from a graffito upon a tomb at Thebes that this reign extended three years and a few months ; we also know that Tut·ankh·Aten followed Smenkh·ka·Re, but we are not certain whether he succeeded from Smenkh·ka·Re or Akh·en·Aten—in other words, whether Tut·ankh·Aten was, for a short time, associated with Akh·en·Aten as co-regent or not. But since his original name has the Aten element, and since the original conception of his secular throne—witness the human arms on the Aten disk, together with the cartouche-names of the Aten and the king (Vol. I, p. 118, Plate II)—is based on pure El Amarna art and Aten worship, one is led to believe that Tut·ankh·Aten was co-regent with Akh·en·Aten for a period.

Introduction

In the tomb of Meryre (II), where we find the historical event, "Tribute of the South brought to the King" dated "year XII," there is an unfinished scene representing this new king, Smenkh·ka·Re and his wife, Mert·Aten. As the mural decorations in this tomb, logically, must have been executed on some subsequent date to year XII, the year XIII–XIV would not be an unreasonable date to fix for the unfinished scene. In the scene of tribute, Mert·Aten is represented unmarried, therefore her marriage with Smenkh·ka·Re must be post that date. In any case, the latest date of Akh·en·Aten's reign is year XVII, the scene of tribute is dated year XII and so many months, we therefore have at most five years in which to place the co-regency of Smenkh·ka·Re, which extended rather more than three years, followed by Tut·ankh·Aten.

As a passing note, one should mention that at the end of Smenkh·ka·Re's reign, there is distinct evidence that the ancient religion of Thebes—the cult of Amen—begins to show itself once more. And that on the so-called ecclesiastical throne of Tut·ankh·Aten, although based on the El Amarna art and Aten worship, the Aten and Amen elements occur side by side in their pristine state (*see* p. 112) ; and upon his secular throne in some cases the Aten element has been erased and the Amen substituted (Vol. I, p. 118).

We clearly see then, from the data recorded, the supremacy of the godly and kingly "Father Aten" could not have been more than ten years or so, namely, from some time in the VIIth to the XVIIth regnal years of Akh·en·Aten.

An inscription upon a box found in Tut·ankh·Amen's tomb, giving (1) the full titulary of Akh·

en·Aten, followed by (2) that of Ankh·khepru·Re Mery·nefer·khepru·Re with the nomen Nefer·nefru· Aten Mery·uan·Re, and (3) the name and titles of the Great-King's-Wife Mert·Aten, is definite evidence of a co-regency between those two kings. The cartouches on the two knobs of the box, namely, " Ankh·khepru·Re, beloved of Nefer·khepru·Re," " Nefer·nefru·Aten, beloved of Uan·Re," prove to whom the box belonged (i.e. Smenkh·ka·Re) ; there would, therefore, be no reason for the joint-titulary of the two kings on the lid, if they had not been associated in a co-regency. And the name and titles of the Great-King's-Wife, Mert·Aten, at the end of that joint-titulary show that Ankh·khepru·Re became king, in accordance with the ancient Egyptian law of succession, by his marriage to the heiress of the kingdom, the crown princess. But who was Ankh· khepru·Re — Smenkh·ka·Re Zeser·khepru ? — whose names, we learn from the above inscription, were changed to Ankh·khepru·Re beloved of Nefer· khepru·Re, etc. There is no document to tell us, but the epithets given to this boy-king, derived directly from Akh·en·Aten's own prenomen, point, at least, to a close kinship, and even suggest that he may have been the king's son. Such an hypothesis is not inconceivable, for it was the custom in the Eighteenth Dynasty to marry princelings by unofficial wives or concubines to their half-sisters by the principal wife, when the principal wife had no surviving son. The few monuments that can be identified as portraying this boy-king, show a likeness to Akh·en· Aten. Another argument may be brought forward. If, from the remarkable structural resemblance of Tut·ankh·Aten to his father-in-law, Akh·en·Aten, he is assumed to be his son by an unofficial wife (which I believe to be the case), it is highly improbable that precedence would have been given to one (Smenkh·ka·Re) who was not his (Akh·en·Aten's) son.

A remarkable stela in the Berlin Museum (No. 17,813) has been supposed to represent Akh·en·Aten and his queen Nefer·titi, but the double-crown worn by the one figure and the *khepres*-crown worn by the other figure, make it clear that we have here represented *two kings*, and not a king and his consort. The royal personages represented are, I believe, undoubtedly Akh·en·Aten and his co-regent Smenkh·ka·Re, or rather Nefer·nefru·Aten Mery·uan·Re, as we should now call him.

As Newberry points out : " The intimate relations between the Pharaoh and the boy as shown by the scene on this stela recall the relationship between the Emperor Hadrian and the youth Antinous." In regard to the love of Akh·en·Aten for the youth, it may be pointed out that Gunn and Woolley noticed a very remarkable fact about Queen Nefer·titi at El-Hawatah (a locality at El Amarna) which perhaps has some bearing on this intimate relationship between the king and the boy. At El-Hawatah, says Woolley,

" as nowhere else, the queen's name has in nearly every case been carefully erased, and that of her eldest daughter, Mert·Aten, written in palimpsest upon the stone, her distinctive attributes had been blotted out with cement, her features re-cut and her head enlarged into the exaggerated skull of the princess royal. . . . The ownership or patronage of the precinct was transformed from mother to daughter either during the former's lifetime or on her death."

It is therefore not improbable that Nefer·titi died about the time of this co-regency. Her death might even have been partly the cause of this marriage taking place.

If Smenkh·ka·Re was enthroned about the xiiith regnal year of Akh·en·Aten, and he was his son, he could not have been older than nine or ten years when he was married to the princess royal, who was about the same age.

Newberry also brings to notice, " There is probably yet another monument which shows Smenkh·ka·Re by the side of his father-in-law, Akh·en·Aten. In 1894 Hekekyan Bey, while digging in the neighbourhood of the great prostrate figure of Rameses ii at Memphis, discovered some fragments of sculpture that dated from the time of the El Amarna kings. One piece, which is now in the Museum of the University of Sydney, Australia, has an inscription upon it which records a temple of Aten at Memphis. A second fragment of sculpture shows a young king holding in his hand an ostrich-feather fan and wearing the double-crown, his brow being surmounted by the uræus ; in front of him we see the forearm and part of the flowing garments of a much larger figure that obviously represented another king. Borchardt has rightly interpreted this scene as showing Akh·en·Aten and his co-regent Smenkh·ka·Re."

That piece of sculpture seems to corroborate the suspicion that Smenkh·ka·Re was but a boy when he ascended the throne as a co-regent. Of his reign dated wine-jar inscriptions found at El Amarna extend up to year ii ; a docket upon an oil-jar is dated year iii ; and the graffito upon a mortuary chapel at Thebes of the *uab*-priest of Amen, named Pere, previously referred to, is dated " year iii, third month of the inundation, day 10." A small slab of limestone, bearing a coloured sculpture of a young king and queen, from El Amarna, and now in the Berlin Museum (No. 15,000), in all probability represents this young king and his wife Mert·Aten.

That pretty well exhausts the facts of Smenkh·ka·Re's ephemeral life gleaned from the monuments. Born probably during the ivth regnal year of Akh·en·Aten, and after a short and obscure reign, at the age of about thirteen he disappears into oblivion, his wife with him, and the throne, or rather as I believe the co-regency, was open to the next claimant, or ultimate heir, Tut·ankh·Aten.·

We have already noticed that the second daughter, Makt·Aten, died unmarried. Thus the third daughter, Ankh·es·en·pa·Aten, became the heiress and she was married to Tut·ankh·Aten (" Living Image of Aten ") as he then was named, the Tut·ankh·Amen (" Living Image of Amen ") with whom we are now so familiar. Just when this marriage took place is open to conjecture. It probably occurred in Akh·en·Aten's lifetime, at the near close of his reign, when Ankh·es·en·pa·Aten had reached an age of about ten, and Tut·ankh·Aten was but a boy of nine.

The balance of evidence afforded by Tut·ankh·Amen's mummy, after a very careful anatomical examination, proves him to have been without doubt a stripling of about eighteen years of age when he died (*see* Vol. II, p. 143 ff.). A piece of linen found in the Valley of the Kings was marked " *The Good God, Lord of the Two Lands, Neb·khepru·Re* (Tut·ankh·Amen), *beloved of Min : Linen of the Year VI,*" but later inscriptions upon wine-jars, discovered in his tomb, dated " *Year IX. Wine of the House-of-*

Tut·ankh·Amen from the Western River," indicate that he reigned at least nine years (*see* p. 147 ff.).

The estimate of his age at the time of his accession is amply confirmed by his portrait head springing from a lotus flower (Plate I), and the statuette upon his gold stick (Vol. II, Plate VII), which represents a chubby little figure having all the appearance of extreme youth ; while the age of his death is corroborated by his gold mask (Vol. II, Frontispiece), which faithfully represents his features and exhibits him as a gentle, refined-looking young man well advanced in his teens.

Of his parentage we have no conclusive evidence ; we are thus left to supposition based on common reason. As it is unlikely that he was a mere commoner, we must assume, in default of better knowledge, that he was of blood royal, and that he had some indirect claim to the throne on his own account. For this we have some justification. The general shape of his head, which is of a very uncommon type, is so like that of his father-in-law, that it is more than probable there was a close relationship in blood between the two kings. In fact, this remarkable similarity makes the probability of blood relationship almost a certainty. When his mummy was unwrapped the first and most striking impression to all present was his remarkable structural resemblance to Akh·en·Aten. And, at the risk of being tedious, I repeat, this strong likeness—too evident to be set down as mere accident—presents the historian of this period with an entirely new aspect ; one which may throw light on the ephemeral Smenkh·ka·Re as well as Tut·ankh·Amen, both of whom, as we know, acquired the throne by marrying daughters of Akh·

Introduction

en·Aten. The obscurity of their parentage becomes intelligible if these two princes were the offspring of an unofficial marriage—an hypothesis by no means improbable since there are precedents for it in the royal family of the Eighteenth Dynasty, i.e. the marriage of princes by second wives or concubines to their half-sisters by the official wife, when she (the official wife) had no surviving son.

There is every reason to believe that Akh·en·Aten had other wives, for Dushratta, the King of Mittanni, in a letter to him, sends greetings to his (Akh·en·Aten's) other wives (*see* Vol. II, p. 113 ff.).

The power of the priestly party of Amen, as we have already seen, in Smenkh·ka·Re's reign, was fast growing. The question of a successor to the throne must then have been a vital one, and we may be sure that intrigue was rampant. Thus, since Queen Nefer·titi had no son, is it not more than probable that a son by a less important marriage would be selected as co-regent and successor? His marriage to the eldest living official daughter would follow as a matter of course.

I should, however, mention that there is another aspect upon the subject which must not be overlooked. The affinity noticeable in Tut·ankh·Amen may have been derived directly from Akh·en·Aten or through Queen Tyi. The peculiar physical traits exhibited throughout these so-called heretics are not to be found in any of the members of the preceding Amen·hetep family, but they are noticeable in certain more intimate, as distinguished from more conventional, portraits of Queen Tyi, from whom Akh·en·Aten seems to have inherited his physical peculiarities. In an inscription upon the granite lions

23

from Gebel Barkhal, which are now in the British Museum (No. 431), Tut·ankh·Amen says he " *Restored the monuments of his father, King of Upper and Lower Egypt, Lord of the Two Lands, Neb·maat·Re, Son-of-Re, Amen·hetep* (III)," etc. Heirlooms, or pieces of family property, such as a gold statuette of Amen·hetep III, upon a neck-chain, and a lock of hair of Queen Tyi, enclosed in a series of miniature coffins simulating a royal burial, were discovered among the funerary equipment in this tomb (*see* p. 86 ff.). These imply a close kinship to those predecessors, a kinship which is noticeable in the profile of Tut·ankh·Amen's gold mask (Vol. II, Plate XXIII) and the Berlin head of a queen, possibly Tyi (Davis, " The Tomb of Queen Tîyi," Plate XXXV). Moreover, we glean from the hunting scarabs of Amen·hetep III, and the funerary equipment of this tomb, that the amusements—the pursuit of the chase—of the young ruler were very like those of Amen·hetep III—tastes which are lacking in the life of Akh·en·Aten. But in the face of such facts there are the following objections. Although Tut·ankh·Amen could be the son of Amen·hetep III, either by Queen Tyi, or by a second wife or concubine, his birth must have taken place during the XXXIXth regnal year of that king. Scenes representing the old king and queen which could easily be after that date, depict in their company only the one daughter, Bakt·Aten. And if he were a son of Amen·hetep III by a second wife or concubine, we are faced with the problem, namely, the physical peculiarities noticeable in Akh·en·Aten and Tut·ankh·Amen, which seem to be inherited from Queen Tyi—in the case of Tut·ankh·Amen probably through her son Akh·en·Aten. It is, I think, more likely that the expression " Father " in the inscription upon the Barkal lions has a totally different meaning, i.e. the synonym used by those ancient Egyptian Pharaohs when speaking of their predecessors, not intended to be taken as emphatically meaning their immediate progenitor.

However, there is a " King's-Son," named Thothmes, mentioned on a whip found in this tomb (*see* p. 97).

Unhappily the Egyptian monuments are singularly reticent with regard to unofficial offspring, but we do notice, especially in pictures such as are found in the mortuary chapels of Parennefer and Ay, at El Amarna, hareem buildings attached to the palace assigned to women and slaves, with sentinels guarding the doors. Here, among the many women-folk are even foreigners, and prominently figured is a girl, slightly older than Mert·Aten, named " The Sister of the King's-Great-Wife, Nefer·titi, Benretmut," who is accompanied by achondroplasic dwarfs (cf. p. 128), humorously named " The Vizier of the Queen, Erneheh," and " The Vizier of his mother, Pare." It may be in those quarters that we must seek the mother of the two boys—Smenkh·ka·Re and Tut·ankh·Amen.

There is yet another point which may throw light upon the subject. One of the highest officers of the state under the sovereign was Ay, and his wife, named Tyi, was " Great Nurse," " Nurse of the Great-King's-Wife, Nefer·titi," " Tutoress of the Goddess " (i.e. the queen), and " The King's Concubine." Among Ay's titles we find him to have been " Vizier," " Bearer of the Fan on the Righthand of the King," " Master of the Horse," " Head of the Companions of the King," and " Divine Father." This last title might imply that the king married a daughter of his. Upon glancing back we notice the self-same title was attained by Yua, a much smaller official, who was the father of Queen Tyi and father-in-law of Amen-hetep III, and looking ahead a little, the first thing we see in the sepulchral-chamber of Tut·ankh·Amen (Vol. II, p. 28), is Ay, as king with royal insignia, officiating before the " Osiris " (deceased) Tut·ankh·Amen, with his title and name, " The Divine Father Ay " enclosed in a royal cartouche—the nomen of the Pharaonic titulary assumed by Ay.

That there was some connecting-link between the boy-king and the official Ay is made manifest by a piece of gold-foil discovered by Mr. Theo. M. Davis in the Valley of the Kings. Embossed upon this piece of gold is a scene representing Tut·ankh·Amen slaying with a falchion a Libyan enemy before the high official " The Divine Father Ay," who extends his left hand towards the king, and holds in his right hand his ostrich-feather fan of office. The king is here named " Lord of the Two Lands, Neb·khepru·Re, giving life like the Sun for ever," and behind him is " The Great-King's-Wife," Ankh·es·en·Amen (formerly called Ankh·es·en·pa·Aten). This scene is unprecedented, for the prescribed rite of slaying an enemy of Egypt is invariably performed by the king before a divinity.

It seems fairly clear that while the ascendancy of the Amen cult at Thebes is noticeable at the end of Smenkh·ka·Re's reign, Aten still prevailed at the royal residence-town, Akh·et·Aten. Witness the picture upon the back-panel of Tut·ankh·Amen's secular throne, which manifestly bears all the attributes of the heresy. Subsequently, to suit the religious vacillations, the Aten element was in some cases expunged and the Amen inscribed in its place (Vol. II, p. 118). Among a number of finger-rings bearing the pre-nomen of Tut·ankh·Amen, found at El Amarna, we find a combined Aten and Amen reading, and upon his ecclesiastical throne the Aten and Amen elements are side by side unchallenged (p. 112). Such data make it conclusive that he began as an Aten wor-shipper, and that the reversion to the orthodox doctrine was gradual in transition and not spon-taneous. It would appear that the final change took place when he abandoned the heretic capital and removed the court back to Thebes; an event which probably took place not long after the death of Akh·en·Aten.

We have therefore every reason to believe that both Tut·ankh·Amen and Ankh·es·en·Amen were but children when they succeeded Akh·en·Aten. The succession was weak, and a hazardous position it must have been for those children at that particular stage of their country's history.

Clearly during the first years of this reign of infants there must have been a power behind the throne. That power was evidently Ay, whom we know from the monuments to have been a very close and personal friend of Akh·en·Aten, and who, no doubt, by becoming regent, secured the throne for himself after Tut·ankh·Amen's death. It may even be that Ay was largely responsible for establish-ing the boy upon the throne. However, with King Ay ends that famous Eighteenth Egyptian Dynasty.

In the Innermost Treasury of this tomb were discovered two complete miniature burials. They contained mummies of two still-born babes (p. 88 ff.).

Both nameless, but buried under their father's name, Tut·ankh·Amen, for they never reached this earth alive ! What that the result of an abnormality on the part of the little Queen Ankh·es·en·Amen, or was it the result of political intrigue ending in crime ? Those are questions, I fear, which will never be answered, but it may be inferred that had one of those babes lived there might never have been a Rameses.

Thus it was that the throne passed into the hands of the Grand Chamberlain and " Divine Father " Ay, who, from a finger-ring recently discovered bearing his cartouche and that of Ankh·es·en·Amen, appears to have allied himself to that little widowed queen. From a stela in the Berlin Museum, he seems to have reigned about four and a half years after the death of Tut·ankh·Amen, when eventually he was supplanted by the famous General Hor·em·heb, the founder of the Nineteenth Egyptian Dynasty.

While writing this note upon these kings of the Eighteenth Egyptian Dynasty, I learn that the University of Chicago Expedition has discovered in the vicinity of Medinet Habou, an inscription giving a date as late as the xxvIIth year, and so many months, of the reign of Hor·em·heb. Professor Breasted, in his " Ancient Records " (Vol. I, p. 43, n.e.) publishes the following note :

" In the reign of Ramses II, in the records of a legal suit, reference is made to legal proceedings in year 59 of Harmhab. As it is evident that Harmhab was not a young man at his accession, it is exceedingly improbable that he reigned nearly 60 years. The highest known date on any monument of his reign is year 21. It is therefore probable that in the early Nineteenth Dynasty, when the chronology for the government files of the immediately preceding reigns were being made up, the series of Ikhnaton and his successors was added to the reign of Harmhab, and the names of the kings at any time implicated in the Aten heresy were swept from the records . . ."

Now, if we exclude the obscure and ephemeral reign of Smenkh·ka·Re, it being a co-regency within the sovereignty of Akh·en·Aten, and if, as we now learn, Hor·em·heb's reign extended well into his xxvıııth regnal year, the following reckoning, if not merely coincidental, is certainly very tempting: The reign of Akh·en·Aten $17\frac{1}{2}$ years, plus that of Tut·ankh·Amen $9\frac{1}{2}$ years, plus the " Divine Father " Ay's $4\frac{1}{2}$ years, plus the reign of Hor·em·heb $27\frac{1}{2}$ years = 59 years.

*   *   *   *   *

To quote Maeterlinck, it would have been easy, in regard to every statement, to have allowed the above text to bristle with footnotes and references. In many instances the letterpress would have been swallowed up by masses of comment, very much like those books we hated so much at school. For this reason I give here a short bibliography of the literature and papers that refer to the above kings implicated in the so-called Aten heresy.

Battiscombe Gunn, *Notes on the Aten and His Names*, " The Journal of Egyptian Archæology," IX, p. 168 ff.; J. H. Breasted, *Ancient Records of Egypt*, Vol. I, p. 43, n.e., Vol. II, pp. 841, 843, 870– 874, 875, n.e., 877, 921 ff.; N. de G. Davies, *Rock Tombs of El Amarna*, Vol. II, p. 43, Plates xxxvıı, xxxvııı, xlı, Vol. III, p. 15 ff., Plates xııı, xvıı, xvııı, Vol. V, p. 28 ff., Plates xxxııı, xxxıv, xxxvı, xlııı, Vol. VI ; N. de G. Davies, *Akhenaten at Thebes*, " The Journal of Egyptian Archæology, IX, p. 146, n. 4 ; A. H. Gardiner, *Egyptian Grammar*, p. 204 ;

Introduction

F. Ll. Griffith, *Papyri, Kahun and Gurob*, 1898, Plate xxxviii ; Lepsius, *Denkmäler*, III, pp. 81, e, 188, i ; P. E. Newberry, *Scarabs*, pp. 170–173, 176 ; P. E. Newberry, *Akhenaten's Eldest Son-in-law, Ankhkheprure*, " The Journal of Egyptian Archæology," XIV, pp. 3–9 ; P. E. Newberry, *King Ay, the Successor of Tutánkhamūn*, "The Journal of Egyptian Archæology," xviii, p. 50 ff. ; *Peet-Wolley, The City of Akhenaten*, p. 123 ; W. M. F. Petrie, *Tell El Amarna*, pp. 32, Plate xv, 118 ; W. M. F. Petrie, *A History of Egypt*, II, pp. 179, 183, 207–209 ; W. M. F. Petrie, *Medum*, p. 37 ; Prisse, *Monuments*, XI, p. 3 ; *Recueil de Traveaux, Egypte*, VI, p. 52, XXXII, p. 88 ; Elliot-Smith, *The Tomb of Queen Tiyi* (*Mr. Theo. M. Davis's Excavations*), p. xxiii ff. ; Daressy, *The Tomb of Harmhabi and Touatänkh-Amanou* (*Mr. Theo. M. Davis's Excavations*), pp. 128, Fig. 4, 134 ff., Fig. 15 ; *Zeitschrift für Ägyptische Sprache*, LV, 20.

THE TOMB OF TUT·ANKH·AMEN

CHAPTER I

THE ROOM BEYOND THE BURIAL CHAMBER
(A TREASURY)

THE time came in the sequence of our work to direct our energies towards the Storeroom beyond the Burial Chamber (*see* Vol. I, p. 223), perhaps in this case better named " The Innermost Treasury."

This room is not more than 15 feet 8 inches, by 12 feet 6 inches square, and 7 feet 8 inches in height. Ingress is by means of a low open doorway cut in the northern end of the west wall of the Burial Chamber. It is of extreme simplicity, there being no attempt at decoration. The four walls and ceiling are unsmoothed, the marks of the final chiselling being still visible upon the rock surfaces. In fact, it is just as those ancient Egyptian masons left it—even the last few flakes of limestone from their chisels lay on the floor.

Small and simple, as it is, the impressive memories of the past haunt it none the less. When, for the first time, one enters a room such as this, the sanctity of which has been inviolate for more than thirty centuries, a sense of reverence, if not of fear is felt on the part of the intruder. It seems almost desecration to trouble that long peace and to break that eternal silence. Even the most insensitive person, passing this inviolate threshold, must surely feel awe and wonder distilled from the secrets and shadows of that Tremendous Past. The very stillness of its atmosphere, intensified by the many inanimate things that fill it, standing for centuries and centuries as pious hands had placed them, creates the sense of sacred obligation which is indescribable and which causes one to ponder before daring to enter, much less to touch anything. Emotions thus aroused, of which the sense of awe is the root, are difficult to convey in words; the spirit of curiosity is checked; the very tread of one's foot, the slightest noise, tends to increase a fear and magnify an unconscious reverence —the intruder becomes mute.

That appeal of the past made one hesitate before venturing to enter and explore, until one remembered that, however much one may respect it, an archæologist's duty is to the present, and it is for him to interpret what is hidden and note whatever steps may lead him to his goal.

The doorway of this room, unlike the others, was not bricked-up or sealed; from it we had a clear view of the contents of the room. Within a few days of its discovery (February 17, 1923), after we had made a brief survey of its contents (Vol. I, pp. 183-186), we purposely closed the doorway with wooden boards, in order that, whilst dealing with the vast material in the Burial Chamber, we might not be distracted or tempted to disturb any of the objects in this little room. That wooden hoarding is now removed, and after four years' patient waiting, our attention is once more directed within. All it holds was again revealed—objects many, both of mystic and of absorbing interest, but mostly of purely funerary nature and of intense religious character.

The Room Beyond the Burial Chamber

Placed in the doorway, practically preventing ingress to the room, was the black figure of the jackal-like dog Anubis, covered with linen, and couchant upon a gilt pylon resting on a sledge with long carrying-poles (Plate II). On the ground within the threshold, and in front of the pylon of Anubis, was a small reed torch with clay brick-like pedestal (Plate LII) bearing an incantation " to repel the enemy of Osiris (the deceased), in whatever form he may come," and behind Anubis, a strange head of a cow (Plate IV,B)— emblems these of the tomb and of the world beyond.

Along the south wall, extending from east to west, stood a large quantity of black, sinister, shrine-like chests (Plate III), all closed and sealed save one, the folding doors of which had fallen apart revealing statuettes of the king, swathed in linen, standing on the backs of black leopards. Since the discovery, imagination faltered at the thought of what those other chests might contain. The time has come when we are soon to know.

Stacked on top of those black chests, without any apparent order, save that their stems all pointed west, were a number of model craft (Plate III), equipped with cabins, look-outs, thrones and kiosks, upon the poop, the amidship, and after-decks ; and in front of the chests, resting upon a wooden model of a granary filled with grain, was another and more elaborate boat with rigging and furled sail (Plate III,A). And underneath those black chests, in the south-west corner, was a huge black oblong box (Plate III,B) containing a figure of Osiris swathed in linen.

On the opposite side, placed parallel with the pylon and sledge of Anubis, was a row of treasure caskets beautifully ornamented with ivory, ebony and gesso-gilt, and some vaulted boxes of plain wood, painted white (Plate IV,B). They contained jewels and other treasures, but one of them, the simplest of all, the lid of which I raised when we first entered the room, contained an ostrich-feather fan with ivory handle—a pathetic but beautiful relic of the boy king, to all appearances perfect as when it left his hands.

Packed along this north side of the room (Plate IV,A) were a number of divers objects : more model craft ; a richly ornamented bow-case ; two hunting chariots, their dismembered parts stacked one upon another in a similar manner to the chariots found in the Antechamber ; in the farthest north-east corner, piled on top of one another, were more wooden boxes, miniature coffins, and ten black wooden kiosks undoubtedly housing the *Shawabti*-figures — the answerers for the dead. Many of these objects had been disturbed.

Unquestionably the thieves had entered this little room, but in their predatory quest they seem to have done little further harm than to open and rifle the treasure caskets and some boxes. Some beads and tiny fragments of jewellery scattered on the floor, the broken seals and displaced lids of caskets, folds of linen hanging from the mouths of the boxes, and here and there an overturned object, were the only evidence visible at first sight of their visit. The robber, or robbers, must have been aware of the nature of the contents of this room, for, with rare exception, only those boxes which held objects of intrinsic value had been disturbed.

Such were the general contents of this little room beyond the Burial Chamber. But a single glance sufficed to show that the principal object of all was at the far end, facing the doorway. For there, standing against the east wall, and almost reaching the ceiling, was a large gilded canopy surmounted with rows of brilliantly inlaid solar cobras (Plate v). This canopy, supported by four square posts upon a sledge, shielded a gilt shrine-shaped chest inscribed with formulæ pertaining to the four genii, or children of Horus. Surrounding this shrine-shaped chest, free-standing on the four sides, were statuettes of the guardian goddesses, Isis, Nephthys, Neith, and Selkit (*see* Vol. I, p. 184). The shrine-like chest shielded the Canopic box, which in turn contained the four receptacles that held the viscera of the dead king.

It is obvious that this collection of objects placed within this room formed part of one great recondite idea, and that each of them has a mystical potency of some kind. As Dr. Alan Gardiner rightly says : " It is necessary to admit without hesitation that the idea of a mystical potency inherent in the image of things is a characteristically Egyptian conception . . ." It is for us to discover what were the respective meanings of these objects and their intended divine mystical powers. Scientific research demands the closest investigation, therefore I trust that I may not be misunderstood when I say that it was no question of showing disrespect to the burial ritual of a vanished theology, and still less of gratifying the excitement of a morbid curiosity, when one disturbed this religious paraphernalia. Our task was to leave nothing unexplored which might add to the sum of our steadily growing knowledge, both archæological and historical, of this deeply interesting and most complicated funerary cult.

However strange, however extensive, this funerary outfit may be, it doubtless belonged to a more or less organized system for the common good of the dead, and was a system of defence against human imaginations, the results of obscure ideas. This association of equipment, in more ways than one, had been created to achieve unknown ends, and very much like the innumerable cells of a living body, they possessed, or were supposed to possess, powers to intervene, should they be called upon, in obedience to an order, who knows whence. They constituted, in fact, a form of self-protection for the future. They were a thoughtful people who made them, and, owing to their Age, could not escape from the blinding influence of traditional custom. Ultra-religious as most of the emblems are, there is to be found among them evidence of the splendid capacities of the race that created them.

To endeavour to grasp the meaning of this little room, I will refer to a papyrus now in Turin: a royal tomb plan discovered in the last century, which is no less than a project for the tomb of Rameses IV. Although that document belongs to a reign some two centuries later than Tut·ankh·Amen, it does throw light upon his tomb. The document is a sketch ground-plan for a Pharaonic tomb, giving elevations of the doorways, the names and dimensions of the different corridors and chambers, with specifications such as: "*being drawn with outlines, graven with the chisel, filled with colours, and completed.*" On the back of the papyrus, among other notes, are more measurements with apparently an initial line or title: "*The measurements of the tomb of Pharaoh, Living, Prosperous, Healthy.*" The difference of certain minor details in this ancient sketch-plan, which do not agree exactly with the tomb of Rameses IV—although the plan coincides with the main details—may be explained by the fact that it was but a project modified when making the actual tomb. Among other details of interest the document refers to " *The House of Gold, wherein One rests*," meaning the Burial Chamber where the deceased Pharaoh is placed to rest ; and we find mention of that chamber " *being provided with the equipment of His Majesty on every side of it, together with the Divine Ennead which is in Duat* " (the Nether World).

The golden or yellow hue of the sepulchral chambers in all the royal Theban tombs, doubtless symbolizes the setting of the Sun-god behind the mountains of the west, hence the appellation " *The House of Gold* " given in the document to that part of the tomb—the Burial Chamber—" *Wherein One rests*." The mention : " *provided with the equipment of His Majesty on every side of it*," evidently refers to the great shrines and to the supports for the pall, that were to be erected over the sarcophagus, which are carefully drawn on the plan in exactly the same order as the golden shrines and pall found in Tut·ankh·Amen's tomb. The final phrase : " *together with the Divine Ennead which is in Duat* " seems to refer to the series of figures of divinities such as we discover contained in those numerous black shrine-like chests placed in the room beyond the Burial Chamber. Judging by the tomb of Seti II, where these figures are depicted, they may either be painted on the walls of the tomb or, as in the case of the Eighteenth Dynasty tombs, be represented in plastic form.

In the more developed plan of the Eighteenth

Dynasty royal tomb, the Burial Chamber comprises a hypostyle hall with steps at the end leading down to a kind of open crypt for the sarcophagus, and four small rooms or treasuries—two of which adjoin the pillared portion and two adjoin the so-called open crypt. In the project of the Burial Chamber of Rameses IV, as well as in the tomb itself, these parts have been modified into one large rectangular chamber with a small corridor at the back having niches and recesses. In the document the small corridor with niches and recesses beyond the Burial Chamber are named : " *The corridor which is as Shawabti-place ; the resting-place of the Gods ; the left* (and right) *hand treasury ; and the treasury of the Innermost.*" Upon the walls of the latter—" *the treasury of the Innermost* " —in the tomb of Rameses IV, canopic-jars, kiosks for *Shawabti*-figures, and other funerary furniture are depicted. However, in the earlier Eighteenth Dynasty tombs the canopic equipment was generally placed at the foot of the sarcophagus.

It therefore becomes fairly clear from the data quoted, and from the collection of material found in this little room beyond the Burial Chamber, that it combines several chambers in one : " *The Shawabti-place ; the Resting-place of the Gods* " ; at least one of the two " *Treasuries* " ; and " *the Treasury of the Innermost.*"

This accounts, more or less, for the heterogeneous collection of objects crowded into this little room. In it we find the canopic equipment belonging essentially to the tomb ; safeguards for the deceased's passage through the Underworld ; and objects that the deceased required for his use in daily life, and hence would continue to require in his future life ; jewellery for his adornment, chariots for his recreation, and servants (*Shawabti*-figures) to carry out any irksome work he might be called upon to do in the Hereafter. Housed in those black shrine-like chests there were statuettes of the king representing him in the act of divine pursuit and various forms of his renewed existence; figures of the gods pertaining to "the entire Ennead" since Pharaoh, like the divinity, must have a college of divine persons to help him through the dangers to which he may be exposed. While the little flame lying at the threshold of the doorway was supposed to hinder "*the sand from choking the tomb and repel the intruder*," there were boats to render the deceased independent of the favours of the "*celestial ferrymen*," or to enable him to follow Re, the Sun-god, on his nocturnal voyage through the interconnecting tunnels of the Underworld, and in his triumphal journey across the heavens. There were also barques, fully rigged and equipped with cabins, symbolizing the funeral pilgrimage; there was a granary filled with grain; a saddle-stone for grinding corn; strainers for the preparation of the exhilarating beverage, beer; and natron for the preservation of mortal and immortal remains. There was even a mock figure representing the regermination of Osiris, the revered god of the dead, who like man suffered death, was buried, and who afterwards rose again to immortal life. There were many symbols, the intention of which is obscure, but they, too, had their uses in some superstitious purpose.

Besides the material just recorded there must have been a wonderful display of riches in those treasure caskets, and would still have been, were it not for the selective activities of the dynastic tomb-plunderers.

CHAPTER II

THE FUNERARY EQUIPMENT FOUND IN THE ROOM
BEYOND THE BURIAL CHAMBER

A FIRM conviction among those ancient Egyptians (says Professor Steindorff) was that life did not end at death, but that man continued to live just as he had lived upon this earth, provided that measures for his protection to usher him through the labyrinth of the Underworld and necessaries for his future existence were assured him. We shall now see from the equipment placed in this room beyond the Burial Chamber at least part of what was considered necessary for his protection and for his future existence.

The magical torch and clay-brick pedestal (Plate LII) found at the entrance of this room, must not be confused with the four brick pedestals with figures that were sealed within recesses in the four walls of the Burial Chamber (Vol. II, p. 37), for those magical figures were found intact hidden in niches in the walls of that chamber. This little clay brick with its tiny reed torch and a few grains of charcoal seem not to have been dropped by mere chance on the floor within the threshold in front of Anubis. The magical formula scratched upon the brick tells us that : " It is I who hinder the sand from choking the secret chamber, and who repel that one who would repel him with the desert-flame. I have set aflame the desert (?), I have caused the path to be mis-

40

taken. I am for the protection of the Osiris [the deceased]."

The figure of the god Anubis, who takes upon himself the form of a kind of black jackal-like dog without gender, who not only presided over the burial rites, but also acted as the vigilant watcher over the dead, was appropriately placed in the open doorway, facing outwards towards the west, to guard against the intruder (*see* Plate II). His position in the tomb was evidently not the result of mere convenience, but was intentional. It enabled him to watch over the Burial Chamber and its occupant, while he also guarded his domain the " Treasury of the Innermost."

This watchful, life-size recumbent figure of the Anubis-animal (Plate VI), carved of wood, and varnished with black resin, rests upon a gilded pylon supported by a gilt sledge with four carrying-poles. He was protected with a linen covering—actually a shirt dated in the seventh year of the reign of Akh· en·Aten. Under this covering his body was draped in a thin gossamer-like linen shawl tied at his throat, and fastened around his neck was a long leash-like linen scarf. This was adorned with a double fillet of blue lotus and cornflowers woven upon strips of pith, twisted into a bow at the back of the neck. Under these, gilded on the neck of the beast, is a collar and another long scarf in facsimile of the linen one just described. His eyes are inlaid with gold, calcite and obsidian; the pectinations of the erect pointed ears are gilt; his toe-nails are of silver.

We have already noticed (Vol. II, p. 32, Plate VI) his curious emblems, like skins full of solutions for preserving or washing the body, hung upon poles, and stood behind the great sepulchral shrines in the Burial Chamber. Here, within his gilded pylon, carefully wrapped in linen and deposited in separate compartments, are further strange symbols belonging to his cult : four blue faience forelegs of a bovine animal, which recall the *whm* word-sign to " repeat " ; two small wooden mummiform figures, like the determinative *wi* for " mummy " ; an anthropomorphic figure of Horus, or maybe Re, in blue faience ; a blue faience squatting figure of the ibis-headed god, Thoth ; a blue faience *wadj* " papyrus column," which may signify to " pour out " from the word *wdjh* ; a wax *bahi*-bird ; some pieces of resin ; and lastly, two calcite cups, one inverted over the other, full of an intimate mixture of resin, common salt, sulphate of soda, and a very small proportion of carbonate of soda (natron).[1] Such objects, if my interpretation be correct, seem to signify the perpetuation of, or belong to, the ritual of mummification. In a fifth and much larger compartment in the pylon were eight large pectoral ornaments. These had originally been wrapped in pieces of linen and sealed, but they, like the symbols in the four smaller compartments, had been disturbed by the thieves in search for more valuable loot. The pectorals possibly comprise the god's jewellery, or perhaps they were worn by his eight priests who carried him in procession to the tomb ?

To depart for a moment from the main subject ; what was the origin of this very interesting Anubis-animal ? To explain it, we are driven to conjectures of varying degrees of possibility. It is possible that it originates from some form of domesticated jackal-

---

[1] Analysed by Mr. A. Lucas.

dog of the primitive Egyptians. It presents characteristics of several of the sub-orders of the canine family. It is represented black; as having a smooth coat; the attenuated form of the greyhound; long, pointed muzzle; long, erect, pointed ears; eye-pupils round; the fore-feet have five toes, and the hind-feet only four; and it has a very long, straight, drooping, bushy, and club-like tail. The majority of these characteristics are those of the domestic dog, but in place of the recurved tail peculiar to the dog, it has the long, straight tail of the fox, club-like in form, which it carries in drooping position like the wolf, jackal, or fox. The numerous representations of this Anubis-animal upon the Egyptian monuments resemble largely the bearing of the jackal, and this specimen gives reason to entertain the idea that it may have been a domesticated form of the jackal crossed with another sub-genus of the canine family. The collar and the scarf-like leash that are invariably represented round its neck also suggest an animal brought under human control. And when one takes into account the qualities of the domesticated canine family—devotion to its master, knowledge and defence of his property, attachment to him until death—it may be the reason why those ancients selected this jackal-like dog as the vigilant watcher over their dead.

I have witnessed two animals resembling this Anubis form of jackal-like dog. The first example was seen by me during the early spring of 1926, when in the desert of Thebes I encountered a pair of jackals slinking towards the Nile valley, as is their custom, in the dusk of the evening. One of them was evidently the common jackal (*C. Lupaster*) in spring pelage; but its mate—I was not near enough to tell whether the male or the female—was much larger, of lanky build, and black! Its characteristics were those of the Anubis-animal, save for one point—the tail was short, like the ordinary jackal. In fact, with the exception of its tail, it appeared to be the very counterpart of the figure found in this room. It may possibly have been a case of melanism, or sport deviating in both colour and form from the normal type, but I must admit that its extraordinary likeness to the Anubis beast brought to my mind the possibility of a throw-back or rare descendant of some earlier species in Egypt (for similar animal see upper register, north wall of the tomb of Baqt; Newberry, "Beni Hasan," Part II, Plate IV). The second example that I saw was in October, 1928, during early morn in the Valley of the Kings. It had precisely the same characteristics as the former example described, but in this case was a young animal from about seven to ten months old. Its legs were lanky; its body greyhound-like; it had a long pointed muzzle, large and erect, pointed, ears; but its drooping tail was comparatively short and of ordinary jackal shape. Long hairs of a lighter colour (greyish) under the body could be detected.

I have made inquiries among the inhabitants of Gurna (Western Thebes) regarding these animals. They tell me that individual examples of this black variety, though very rare, are known to them, and that they are always far more attenuated—" of the Selakhi [a kind of greyhound] form "—than the ordinary species.

Characteristics of the Anubis beast are often very noticeable among a black species of the native Egyptian dogs, but like all the Egyptian pariahs they have a curled tail, coiled tightly over the rump, and never straight and drooping like that of the Anubis jackal-like dog.

The fact that this animal is invariably represented genderless suggests the possibility of its being an imaginary beast. On the other hand this want of gender may derive origin from certain precautionary measures " to prevent indignities from being offered " to the dead, mentioned by Herodotus (Book II, p. 89) when describing the ancient Egyptian method of embalming and the embalmers.

Anubis, whose cult was universal in Egypt, was the Totem god of the xviith nome, Cynopolis, of Upper Egypt, as well as in capitals of the xviiith and probably the xiith and xiiith nomes of the same kingdom. And as the custom of embalming the dead gradually developed, he became the patron divinity of that art.

Placed between the fore-feet of this figure of Anubis was an ivory palette (Plate xxii,A) inscribed : " *The royal daughter, Mert·Aten, beloved and born of the Great-Royal-Wife, Nefer·neferu·nefer·titi.*" Mert· Aten was married to Smenkh·ka·Re, who preceded Tut·ankh·Amen. It contained six partially-used colours : white, yellow, red, green, blue, and black. Although samples obtainable without damaging so precious an article were insufficient for confirmatory tests to be applied, Mr. Lucas was of the opinion that the white was probably calcium sulphate, the yellow of the nature of orpiment (sulphate of arsenic), the red an ochre, and the black carbon. The green was not examined and the blue was mostly used up.

Immediately behind the pylon of Anubis, and facing west, was the golden head of the Meh·urit cow (Plates IV,B, LIX,A), called "*The Eye of Re.*" This, apparently, is a form of the goddess Hathor as Mistress of Amentit, the "Land of Sunset," who receives in her Mountain of the West the sinking sun and the dead. Around her neck was tied a linen covering, knotted at the throat. She is carved of wood ; her horns are made of copper ; and her inlaid eyes of lapis lazuli glass take the form of the "Eye of Re," from which she derives her name. Her head, ears and part of her throat are gilded, symbolizing the golden rays of the setting sun ; the remainder of her neck, like the pedestal upon which she rests, is varnished with black resin, representing the gloom of the vale of the Underworld out of which her head protrudes.

Standing on the floor behind the head of the cow and before the Canopic equipment, were three alabaster (calcite) *tazzas* supporting shallow alabaster dishes (Plate IV,B), two of which were covered with similar inverted bowls. The central dish, which may have contained water, was empty, but the covered dishes on the right and left contained, according to Mr. Lucas, a mixture in powder composed of fine crystals of natron, some common salt, and a small proportion of sulphate of soda. Their significance is not understood, but the materials they contained suggest that they had something in common with the ritual of mummification.

The next in sequence of the arrangement of objects in this little room, and also the most effective, was the Canopic equipment—a monument not easily forgotten, that stood before the centre of the east

end wall, immediately opposite the entrance doorway (Plate v). It was some 6 feet 6 inches in height,
and it occupied a floor area of some 5 by 4 feet. Even
though it was possible to guess the purport of this
monument, its simple grandeur, the calm which
seemed to accompany the four little gracious statuettes
(Plates VII, VIII) that guarded it, produced a mystery
and an appeal to the imagination that would be
difficult to describe. The shielding canopy overlaid
with gold was supported by four corner posts upon
a massive sledge, its cornice surmounted with brilliantly inlaid solar cobras ; on each side was a lifelike
gilded statuette of a tutelary goddess, guarding her
charge with outstretched protective arms. The central portion—a large shrine-shaped chest—also completely overlaid with gold and surmounted with
solar cobras, concealed a smaller chest hewn out of
a solid block of veined semi-translucent alabaster
(calcite). This alabaster chest, with gilt dado,
covered with a linen pall (Plate IX), and standing
upon a silver-handled gesso-gilt wooden sledge, held
the four receptacles for the viscera of the king. The
viscera, wrapped in separate mummiform packages,
were contained in four miniature gold coffins.

These observations bring us to consider the
meaning of this elaborate Canopic equipment. In
the Egyptian process of mummifying the body, the
viscera were separately preserved in four receptacles
associated with the genii Imsety, Hepy, Dua·mutef,
and Qebeh·snewef, who were under the special protection of Isis, Nephthys, Neith, and Selkit. Each
of these four tutelary goddesses was supposed to
have possessed within herself a genius, which it was
her duty to protect. Hence we find Imsety guarded

by Isis, and Hepy by Nephthys; the guardians of
Dua·mutef and Qebeh·snewef were Neith and Selkit
respectively. An ancient myth connected with the
four genii, said to be the sons of Horus, tells us that
they arose from water in a lily, and that the crocodile
god, Sebekh, commanded by the Sun-god Re, had
to catch them in a net. However, it is also said that
Isis produced them, and that they succoured Osiris
in his misfortunes, and saved him from hunger and
thirst, and hence it became their office to do the same
for the dead. From the myth, and from the logical
procedure in mummification, came the peculiar conception, which already shows itself in the Old and
Middle kingdoms, and was universally accepted in
the New Empire. By the intervention of these genii
the viscera were prevented from causing the deceased
any unpleasantness. The viscera were removed from
the body and placed in the charge of these genii
guarded by their respective goddesses whose actual
spirits they were. Hence, after the mummy, its
coffins, sarcophagus, and covering shrines, the most
important among the funeral appurtenances was the
Canopic equipment for the viscera. And in this instance the Canopic chest, with its protective goddesses
and coverings, was in keeping, both in richness and
in glory, with the exalted station of its owner.

The alabaster Canopic chest (Plate IX) certainly
proves to be one of the most beautiful objects among
the funerary equipment of the king. Shrine-like in
form, it has the usual entablature common to the
design, its sides have a slight " batter " and on the
corners the four guardian goddesses are carved in
high-relief—Isis on the south-west corner, Nephthys
on the north-west corner, Neith on the south-east

corner, and Selkit on the north-east corner. On each side are their respective formulæ in bold hieroglyphics, incised and filled in with dark blue pigment. The massive lid, which forms the entablature, was carefully secured to the chest by means of cord bound to gold staples and sealed (Plate LIII,A) with the design : a recumbent figure of the Anubis jackal-like beast over the nine races of mankind in prisoner form, in fact, the device of the royal necropolis seal. The dado, overlaid with thin sheet-gold, is embossed with *ded* and *thet* symbols probably denoting the protection of both Isis and Osiris. The interior of the chest was only carved out some five inches deep, but sufficiently to give the appearance of four rectangular compartments containing each a jar (Plate LIII,B). Covering the tops of each of the imitation jars were separate human-headed lids, finely sculptured in alabaster in the likeness of the king (Plate x). The two on the east side faced west, and the two on the west side faced east. The rebated flanges of the human-headed lids fitted into the openings of the counterfeit jars : that is to say they covered the mouths of the four cylindrical holes in the chest which took the place of real jars. In each hollow, wrapped in linen, was an exquisite miniature gold coffin (Plate LIV), elaborately inlaid and resembling the second coffin of the king. They were placed upright, facing in the same direction as the alabaster lids ; they had been subjected, like the king's mummy, to unguents which had solidified and stuck them fast to the bottom of the hollows. Whether this anointing took place in the tomb or elsewhere, we were unable to find sufficient evidence to make any final decision. The only possible suggestion that it might

E

have taken place beforehand was the fact that the human-headed lids were slightly displaced—a displacement which might have occurred from jolting during transport to the tomb. There was, however, sufficient evidence to show that the anointing commenced with the south-east coffin, thence to the south-west coffin, the north-west coffin and ending by the north-east coffin, when a very little of the unguent was left.

These miniature coffins (Plate LIV) which held the viscera are wonderful specimens of both goldsmith's and jeweller's art. They are replicas of the second coffin that enclosed the king, but far more elaborately inlaid in feather design, the burnished gold faces being the only part of the figures that has been left plain. Each bears down the front the formula pertaining to the goddess and her genius to which it belongs, and each has on the interior surfaces beautifully engraved texts pertaining to the rite.

But in spite of all this care and costly expenditure to preserve and to protect the mortal remains of the young king, the sumptuous funerary equipment, and what must have been elaborate religious rites at the time of entombment, we find gross carelessness on the part of those people who undertook the obsequies. They must have known better than we do now, that the goddess Nephthys should be on the south side of the chest, and that her charge was the genius Hepy. And that Selkit should be on the east side, and her charge was the genius Qebeh·snewef. Yet in erecting this Canopic equipment, even though it bears distinct marks as well as distinguishing inscriptions upon each side, they placed Selkit south in the place of Nephthys, and Nephthys east where Selkit should have been. Moreover, the carpenters, who put together the sections of the canopy and fitted the wooden covering over the alabaster chest, left their refuse (chips of wood) in a heap on the floor of the chamber.

We will now turn to those sinister black chests and boxes that were stacked along the whole of the south side of the room (Plate III). Hitherto, imagination faltered at the thought of what they might contain; with suppressed excitement we opened them one by one: they each enclosed one or more figures of gods or of the king.

No pains were spared in making and housing these figures. They were placed in twenty-two black wooden shrine-shaped chests constructed upon wooden sledges. Each chest had folding doors carefully closed and fastened with cord and seal. Their seals, made of Nile mud probably mixed with a small quantity of oil, bore an impression of the necropolis seal in miniature: a recumbent figure of the jackal-like dog, Anubis, over nine prisoner foes, disposed in three rows of three, which, according to Dr. Alan Gardiner, represent the nine races of mankind, called by the ancient Egyptians " The Nine Bows "—a device signifying the protection of the vigilant Anubis against all human enemies. Each statuette was enveloped in a piece of linen from the looms of Akh·en·Aten, which date back as early as the third year of that reign—rather more than twenty years before the burial of Tut·ankh·Amen. But although each statuette was enveloped in linen, their faces without exception were carefully left uncovered, and many of the gods had tiny fillets of real flowers fastened round their heads (Plate xi). These fillets in many instances had fallen from decay over their shoulders.

The statuettes themselves are beautifully carved of a hard wood, overlaid with gesso and thin sheet-gold; their eyes are inlaid with obsidian, calcite, bronze, and glass; the details of their head-dresses, collars, and garments, are carefully wrought; the insignia upon the crowns and emblems in the hands of the figures of the king are made of bronze plated with thin sheet-gold; and each statuette, whether of the king or of a god, stands upon an oblong pedestal varnished with black resin. The gods have their names painted in yellow upon their pedestals, and these figures display all the charms of the Eighteenth Dynasty art. The statuettes of the king are realistically sculptured; some show a physical likeness to Akh·en·Aten.

Including the two that were found in the Antechamber (Vol. I, p. 114), there were thirty-four in all: twenty-seven of divinities and seven of the king.

The exact meaning as well as the presence of this series of figures in the tomb is not clear to us. It may be that some, if not all of the divinities comprise " *the Divine Ennead which is in Duat* " (the Nether World), or it may be they represent the Ennead—the divine tribunal or synod of gods—associated with the struggle between Horus and Seth, for two of the statuettes of the king obviously pertain to that myth, while the others seem to represent him in various forms of his future existence, to show that he " *die not a second time in the Nether World.*"

The figures of the divinities include the Sun-god Atum; Shu, the god of the atmosphere; the Earth-god, Geb; the goddesses Isis and Nephthys; Horus the Elder; Horus within the shrine; Ptah, the patron deity of Egypt (Plate LV,B); Sekhmet, the lion goddess of war (Plate LV,A); Ta·tenen, (?) a special form of Ptah; Khepre, regarded as a form of the Sun-god; Mamu (Plate LVI,C), Sent, and Ta·ta; the children of Horus, Imsety (Plate LVI,B), Hepy, Dua·mutef (? two figures), and Qebeh·snewef; Menkaret (Plate LVII), who holds the king above her head; two standards of Seshet, the goddess of writing; the falcon standard of Spedu (Plate LVIII,B); the falcon standard of Gemehsu (Plate LVIII,A); a serpent divinity named Neter·ankh (Plate LIX,B); all by whom the king is beloved, and two Ihy-musicians (Plate LVI,A).

The only black figures (i.e. covered with a black resin), so numerous in the preceding royal tombs of this dynasty, were the two (?) Ihy-musicians resembling the infant Horus (Plate LVI,A). They bear no inscriptions, but they hold in their outstretched right hands a gilded emblem of Hathor, and may possibly be identified with the Ihy-musicians of Hathor in the Nether World, who worshipped that goddess and the name of her son. This Ihy being is mentioned in the " Book of the Dead " in connexion with the " *Negative Confessions*," numbering forty-two, " *Said on arriving at the Hall of Righteousness*," so that the deceased may be freed of his sins and that " *he may look upon the Divine Countenance*." A parallel to these two figures may be found in a scene in a tomb in the necropolis of Meir and in the tomb of Amenemheb at Thebes, where not only female musicians of Hathor but Ihy-musicians participate in the festival of Hathor in some connexion

53

with the deceased. Another remarkable group represents the Osirian king being held above the head of the god, or goddess, Menkaret (Plate LVII). The king is here attired as Osiris wearing the crown of Lower Egypt. His close-fitting winding-sheet confines his arms, hands, body, legs and feet. The divinity, Menkaret, seemingly lifts him up to enable him to greet the Sun-god. Underlying this group is the character of that ancient nation, living as it was under the influence of an innocent form of superstition, the worship of the glorious luminary, their symbol of both the might and beneficence of the Master of the Universe.

The statuettes of the king show the influence of the El Amarna school. In the modelling of these particular figures, even though they be of repeated traditional type, there is a direct and spontaneous feeling for nature. The feeling here exhibited is beyond the formalized conventions learnt by rote; they show both energy and grace, in fact, the divine and the human have been brought in familiar touch with one another. Two of them depict the young Pharaoh standing with left foot forward. He wears the crown of Lower Egypt, the *usekh*-collar with *mankhet*, the pleated *shendyt*-kilt, and sandals. In one instance he holds in his left hand the long crooked *awt*-staff, and in his right the flagellum (Plate XII,A); in the second figure, in place of the crooked staff, he holds a long straight stick (Plate XII,B). In a third and slightly larger example, the king, in precisely the same attitude and holding the crooked *awt*-staff and flagellum, wears the crown of Upper Egypt (Plate XII,C). Another pair of statuettes represent the king upon papyrus-reed floats, and appear to

symbolize a mythical pursuit : Tut·ankh·Amen as
the youthful warrior Horus killing the Typhonial
animal, the hippopotamus, in the marshes (Plates
XIII, LX). These two figures, exactly similar, are
remarkable for the vigour and animation they display. They picture the king in the act of hurling
a javelin. He wears the Lower Egyptian crown and
in his left hand holds the coil of cord used with the
javelin or harpoon.

From the myth of Horus, sculptured on the walls
of the temple of Edfu, we gather some knowledge
as to the meaning of these two figures. Apparently
the divinity took upon himself the form of a young
man of superhuman stature and physique, who
wielded a javelin twenty cubits in length with chain
of over sixty cubits, as though it were a reed. Horus
hurled this mighty weapon and struck the great
hippopotamus, Seth, who lurked in the waters to
destroy him and his followers, when the storm came
that would wreck their boats. Thus did Horus, the
avenger, defeat the abominable one, the enemy of
Osiris. However, we also glean from the myth that
the great battle is not yet, but that Horus will destroy Seth, when Osiris and the gods will again reign
upon this earth. Moreover a passage from the
account of " *the Contendings of Horus and Seth*," in
a recently discovered papyrus, dating from the reign
of Rameses V, throws further light upon this repre-
sentation of the king impersonating, in divine attri-
bution, Horus : " *Therefore they went into their ships
in presence of the Ennead. Thereupon the ship of
Seth sank in the water. And Seth changed himself into
a hippopotamus, and he caused to founder the ship of
Horus. Thereupon Horus took his barb, and threw*

55

it at the Majesty of Seth."[1]   It is also of interest to observe that at a much later date—the Hellenistic period in Egypt—we find Horus as a warrior, represented on horseback attacking his foe, a crocodile, with a lance, very similar to and possibly the prototype of St. George and the Dragon of the Christian era.   The frail reed float upon which the king stands, is painted green and has gilt calices and bindings at the stem and stern.   Such floats were obviously made of bundles of papyrus-reeds or rushes lashed together—a primitive form of craft used both for hunting in the marshes, and for ferrying purposes, in past ages as well as by the inhabitants of the upper reaches of the Nile to-day (*see* Plate LXII).

Perhaps even more mysterious are the two figures representing the king upon the backs of leopards (Plate XIV).   In both cases Tut·ankh·Amen wears the White Crown of Upper Egypt, the *shendyt*-kilt, sandals, and in his hands he holds the straight-staff (with umbel) and the flagellum.   He stands upon a pedestal which is fixed upon the back of a black leopard, having its facial markings and internal pectinations of its ears gilt.   Fragments of similar figures found in the tombs of preceding Eighteenth Dynasty monarchs clearly show that these extraordinary figures are not unusual in Pharaonic funerary equipment, but no light as yet has been thrown upon their meaning.   The leopards are rendered in the attitude of walking, hence suggesting movement, as if the king was about to enter, or pass out from, the Underworld.

There was a flotilla of model craft.   Fourteen

[1] Alan H. Gardiner, "The Chester Beatty Papyrus, No. 1," Chap. 13, ll. 9 and 10.

were put on the top of those twenty-two black shrine-shaped chests that housed the statuettes, a fully rigged model was stood upon a miniature granary in front of the chests, another rigged model in the north-west corner, and two others were placed in convenient places on the north side of the room (*see* Plates III, IV). All the model craft on the south side had their bows towards the west. Two on the north side of the room had been overturned by the thieves. The remainder of this group were discovered in the Annexe—unfortunately these were almost entirely broken up through ill-usage at the hands of the plunderers.

Among these craft we find models to follow the voyage of the sun; canoes for hunting the hippopotamus and fowling in the Hereafter, symbolizing the mythical pastimes of Horus in the marshes; vessels for the holy pilgrimage to and from Abydos; and craft to render the deceased independent of the favours of the "*celestial ferrymen*" to reach the "*fields of the blessed*," that are surrounded by seething waters difficult to traverse. Some, we are told, would hope to be carried over by the favour of the divine birds—the falcon of Horus, the ibis of Thoth —others pray to the four heavenly spirits, Imsety, Hepy, Dua·mutef, and Qebeh·snewef, to bring them a ferry-boat; or they turn to the Sun-god himself, that he should carry them over in his barque. But here, by the mythical potency inherent in these models, the king is rendered independent.

These models are made out of logs of wood, pinned together, shaped and planed with the adze. They arc painted and gilt and in some instances highly decorated with brilliant ornamentation. With

57

the exception of a model reed canoe, they appear to represent carvel-built boats, with planking flush, i.e. planks or blocks of timber laid edge to edge so that they present a smooth surface without, fastened on the inside with tree-nails, having no ribs, but thwarts or cross-ties to yoke the sides, the side planking being fixed fore and aft to the stem and stern pieces. They have a steering-gear consisting of two large paddles which operate upon upright crutches and overhanging cross-beams before the poop-deck.

The four ships (two large and two small) to follow the divine journeys of the sun (Plate LXI,A), represent a kind of light craft probably developed from the primitive reed-float. They have a round bottom, slightly flattened under the bow and stern; their two ends gradually rise in a fine curve, the stem turned up and ending in an upright papyrus shaped post, the stern-post bent back and terminating in a papyrus pillar; in fact, in their general shape, they remind one of the Venetian gondola. Amidships is the gilded throne for the royal passenger, named on the larger barques " Beloved of Osiris," " Beloved of Sokar," and on the smaller " Like Re," " Giving Life." Thus the deceased journeys as companion of Re, the Sun-god, by day over the heavenly ocean, by night through the realms of Osiris.

" During the daytime," says Professor Maspero, " the pure Soul was in no serious danger; but in the evening, when the eternal waters which flow along the vaulted heavens fall in vast cascades adown the west and are engulfed in the bowels of the earth, the Soul follows the barque of the Sun and its escort of luminary gods into a lower world bristling with ambuscades and perils. For twelve hours, the divine squadron defiles through long gloomy corridors, where numerous genii, some hostile, some

friendly, now struggle to bar the way, and now aid it in sur-
mounting the difficulties of the journey. Great doors, each
guarded by a gigantic serpent, were stationed at intervals, and
led to an immense hall of flame and fire, peopled by hideous
monsters and executioners, whose office it was to torture the
damned. Then came more dark and narrow passages, more blind
gropings in the gloom, more strife with malevolent genii, and
again the joyful welcoming of the propitious gods. At midnight
began the upward journey towards the eastern regions of the
world ; and in the morning, having reached the confines of the
Land of Darkness, the sun emerged from the east to light another
day."

The two craft (?) for the celestial ferry (Plate
LXI,B) are very similar in type to the last, but they
have the stem and stern turned inwards : the two
ends, which rise high out of the water in a beautiful
curve, are bent back and end in the familiar papyrus
umbel. They have a broad beam and would seem
to be capable of navigating shallow water with mini-
mum draught and maximum load. The gods of
the four cardinal points are said to have placed four
such craft, called " *sekhen*," for the ascent of Osiris
to the sky. The barques for the divine journeys of
the sun and these craft for ferrying to the fields of
the blessed, by being intended for divine purpose,
were towed or propelled by supernatural agency, and
therefore did not require sail or oar.

The canoe for the mythical pastimes of Horus
(Plate LXII,A) is a model of a very primitive form
of craft, since from its details it was evidently made
of bundles of papyrus stalks lashed together at intervals into canoe-shape. The bow and stern rise slightly
and end in conventional umbels of papyrus. The
primitive reed-float (Plate LXII,B), from which this
kind of craft is derived, although no longer found

in Egypt proper, still survives in Nubia and in the upper reaches of the Nile. A form of reed craft similar to our model is invariably depicted in fowling, fishing, and harpooning scenes, found among the mural paintings of private tomb-chapels of the Old and Middle Kingdoms, and of the New Empire, where it is called the " *wsekhet* "-boat. Such scenes, I believe, are as mythical as the pastimes of Horus. However, " Plutarch tells us that the hippopotamus was a Typonian animal, so that the hunting of the hippopotamus would naturally evoke the memory of the struggle between Horus and Seth." [1]

Four of the series of funeral boats have a midship-mast, rigging, and a square sail (Plate LXIII,A). Amidships is an ornately decorated cabin, and on the forecastle and poop-decks a gilded pavilion. Although these vessels have a peculiar pointed stem and a fish-tail stern, they recall to mind the " *Nagga* " still plying on the Nile in Nubia, which is constructed of blocks of acacia wood pinned together with tree-nails on the inside, and is no doubt the direct descendant of these older craft. The remaining seven craft belonging to this series are without sail or oar (Plate LXIII,B). They also appear to be models of carvel-built boats ; the stem and stern pieces are curved upward and terminate with blunt ends. Upon the overhanging forecastle and poop-decks are small " look-outs," and amidships a large double roofed, elaborately decorated cabin showing doors and windows. This last series of eleven craft was evidently intended for the pilgrimage to the holy spot, Abydos, where the deceased king should take some part in connexion with the funerary festivals of

---

[1] Davies and Gardiner, " The Tomb of Amenemhēt," p. 30.

Osiris. By causing him to enjoy similar funeral rites he was identified with that great god of the dead; in the same manner, the king, by following the solar course, was identified with the Sun-god. It is problematical whether the procession up and down stream ever occurred, or whether it had any objective reality; for if it did occur, why were these models placed in the tomb?

Perhaps one of the most curious objects among this funerary equipment was found in a large oblong box in the south-west corner of the room, under some of the shrine-shaped chests (Plates III, LXIV,B). This object, commonly known to us as a germinated figure of Osiris, or Osiris-bed, comprises a wooden frame moulded in the form of that god, hollowed out, lined with linen, filled with silt from the Nile bed, and planted with corn (Plate LXIV,A). This was moistened; the grain germinated, and the inanimate form became green and living; thus symbolizing the resurrection of Osiris and of the deceased. This life-size effigy was completely wrapped in linen winding-sheets and bandaged in the like manner as a mummy. It is but another example how, in that ancient funerary cult, the virtuous dead were identified in every possible way with Osiris.

Symbolical of brewing the divine beverage, beer, for the god, were two strainers that were placed upon one of the chests. These are made of wood, covered with a coat of gesso, and have central disks of copper pierced with numerous small holes for straining purposes (Plates III, LXV,A).

Doubtless the ancient and modern Egyptian process of brewing, or making " Booza " as it is now called, was much the same. This primitive form of beer seems to be made as follows : yesterday's bread—wheat, barley or maize—is crumbled into a large vessel, and covered with water, and left for a period of three days. A comparatively small measure of grain is placed in a bowl and covered with hot water, and left for a day. After this, the water is removed by straining, and the grain is dried in the sun for one day, when a milky-white exudation caused by incipient germination occurs. The grain at this stage is then powdered into a meal, and is mixed with the first preparation, and left for a period of about ten hours. This mixture (i.e. the first and second preparations) is afterwards vigorously kneaded, the liquid being strained from it into a fresh vessel ready for drinking, thus forming in its completed state a turbid alcoholic liquor rather stronger than common beer. The solid refuse is generally thrown away, although occasionally it is eaten by the lower classes, flavoured with red pepper, or sometimes given pure to horses.

In a rough wooden box was a model " *Mola Trusatilis* " or thrusting hand-mill for grinding corn into a coarse meal (Plate LXV,B). It consists of a saddle-stone and muller made of yellow quartzite (a sort of crystalline sandstone) ; the saddle-stone is let into a wooden seat with a trough to receive the meal, and is coated with gesso ; the muller, oval and flat-bottomed, was used for rubbing the grain upon the saddle-stone into meal.

Burchardt in his " Travels in Nubia " (1822), while mentioning the people of Berber, says :

" As they have no mills, not even hand-mills, they grind the dhoura (a local millet) by strewing it upon a smooth stone, about two feet in length and one foot in breadth, which is placed in a sloping position before the person employed to grind. At the lower extremity of the stone, a hole is made in the ground to contain a jar, wooden bowl, or some such vessel, which receives the dhoura flour. The grinding is effected by means of a small stone flat at the bottom ; this is held in both hands, and moved backwards and forwards on the sloping stone by the grinder, who kneels to perform the operation."

This lucid description of what was no less than a saddle-stone and muller, such as we have before us, and the method adopted for grinding the corn, leaves little doubt that this ancient model is, though less primitive, a prototype. Women are shown using this form of hand-mill in the chapel of Amenemhēt, and men similarly occupied in the chapel of Baqt, at Beni Hasan.[1] This kind of hand-mill was obviously employed for grinding flour for bread, and although the grinding of the flour was the peculiar duty of women and menials, I believe I am right, when I say it was the privilege of the Pharaoh to prepare the meal for the deity. He was, moreover, actually the divine triturator.

It is remarkable how this funerary equipment retains survivals of earlier burial customs, which have long ceased to exist in private tombs, namely, models of boats, figures and implements of domestic nature —here possibly for divine purpose. Another of these models takes the form of a miniature granary (Plate LXV,C), showing a doorway to an enclosure with entrance yard and sixteen separate compartments for cereals, which were found filled to the brim with grain and seeds. Large " *Shunas* " of this kind, built of sun-dried mud bricks, are the mode for storing cereals in Egypt to-day. Their external architectural

[1] Newberry, " Beni Hasan," Part I, Plate XII ; Part II, Plate VI.

details are precisely the same as this very model of thirty-three centuries ago.

As this completes the material that was placed on the south side of the room, I will now turn to the objects placed on the north side.

Here, placed parallel with the pylon of Anubis and reaching as far as the Canopic equipment, was a row of treasure caskets and plain white boxes (Plate IV). Unfortunately this group had been attacked by the dynastic tomb-plunderers for the more valuable gold and silver articles that the caskets and boxes had contained. Their seals were broken, their contents ransacked, their pieces of greater value stolen; moreover, the remainder of their contents was left in utter disorder.

It may be here remarked that valuable woods and ivory, natural stones, faience, glass and metals were employed by the ancient Egyptians for the manufacture and decoration of their caskets. Throughout the East, through all ages, these highly ornamental boxes were used to hold the more valuable and personal belongings—trinkets and clothes—or as repositories for cosmetics in costly vessels. In fact, to this day, the pride of the fellah is the gaudily bespangled and more than often trumpery box, in which he keeps his most treasured articles.

With the ancient Egyptian examples of boxes there was never any attempt at secret contrivances —hidden compartments or false bottoms—such as are often found in chests of the sixteenth and seventeenth centuries of our era. They have always simple interiors which are sometimes divided by partitions for special purposes. Such boxes rank among the most ancient domestic furniture, and in all probability precede the bedstead, couch and chair. They may be said to be the ancestors of the " chest-of-drawers," of which the later Oriental spice and inlaid medical chests enclosing sets of small drawers are but the transitional form. Boxes and caskets were in dynastic times an almost universal possession; with the rich they were often, as we see, of great value, with the poor accordingly plain and simple. They were almost invariably for domestic purpose; nothing in the nature of an ancient Egyptian " strong-box " has been found. There were no locks, there-fore anything like a " strong-box " was useless, since the means of closing it depended on string and seal.

Although hinges were known to the Egyptians— several examples having been found on boxes in this tomb—they were rarely employed for attaching the lid to the box. A movable lid, separate from the box, was generally the fashion. The substitute for a hinge employed to hold the lid to the back of the box is ingeniously simple : two small holes, a slot, or a rebate, in the interior of the upper part of the back of the box, were made to receive corresponding projections on the cross-battens of the underside of the lid, which when lowered and slid into position prevented the back of the lid from being raised. The forepart of the lid was then held down by means of cord tied round the knob on the top of the lid and on the front of the box, which in turn was secured by a seal. Thus, unless the seal was broken and the cord severed, the lid was held firmly to the box at the back and front.

As a result of this ancient custom of securing goods, it is not surprising to find the more valuable and personal equipment of the king, whether it be funerary or otherwise, stored in highly ornamental caskets and boxes. Many magnificent examples have been found in this tomb, and in this treasury, among a group of six, we have before us four specimens showing very fine workmanship, especially so in the manner of marquetry-inlay, in which over 45,000 pieces of inlay have been employed in the ornamentation of a single specimen (*see* Plate xv,B).

The first casket, which stood nearest the doorway, is embellished with an ivory and ebony veneer and marquetry-inlay : namely, a great number of small pieces of ivory and ebony arranged to form diamond, criss-cross, and herring-bone patterns within panels formed by a veneer of broad and narrow strips of ivory and ebony. The casket is oblong in shape, stands upon four square feet, and has a vaulted lid (Plate xv,B). As is usual in all such cases of cabinet-maker's art, the basic wood of the casket is of poorer quality, possibly of the genus tamarix, and over this inferior body the valuable ivory and ebony veneer and marquetry-inlay have been laid by means of an adhesive : that is to say, the external surfaces of the body were prepared, made perfectly smooth, and a film of glue applied and the veneer and marquetry laid on. After these had been pressed and allowed to dry thoroughly, their upper surfaces were, in turn, smoothed and polished. This class of decoration is also found on ceremonial " snake " sticks (Vol. II, Plate viii,B), made probably by the same artisan. A docket written in hieratic upon the lid of the casket reads : " *Jewels of gold of the procession made in the bed-chamber*[1] *of Neb·khepru·Re* (Tut·ankh·Amen)." It

[1] In my opinion " bed-chamber " may possibly refer to the " bier-chamber."

contained a lot of mixed jewellery, some of which may have belonged to other caskets, the thieves having taken the pieces of greater value and left the rest in disorder.

The second casket (Plate xvi) is of unusual shape, as it takes the oval form of a cartouche. It is constructed of a reddish-brown wood of possibly coniferous nature and is bordered in veneer fashion with strips of ebony. Around its sides are three horizontal bands of hieroglyphic script, engraved and filled in with blue, giving the titulary and other designations of the king. But the lid is its real and striking feature : it is one huge cartouche bearing finely carved ebony and stained ivory characters of the nomen of Tut·ankh·Amen ; and these characters are laid upon a rich gold ground bordered with black ebony, which in turn is inlaid with ivory-white details and designations of the king (Plate xvi,A). Like the first casket its contents had been ransacked. We found in it but a confused residue of jewellery, a mirror-case, and some sceptres of sovereignty ; the sceptres probably belonged to it.

The third was but a plain whitened wood box with vaulted lid. It was empty save for a pair of fancy leather sandals of slipper-like form, and a stone anklet. It possibly contained vestments, parts of which were found in the other caskets.

The fourth and larger casket (Plate xvii,B) is made of a coniferous wood and ornamented with broad rails and styles of veneered ivory. Its panels formed by the rails and styles are decorated with an applied fretwork of gilt wood symbols—*ankh, uas,* and *neb* signs —a formula meaning " All Life and Good Fortune." The gilding of these open-work symbols in contrast to the dark brown colour of the basic wood and the white ivory rails and styles gives a very rich and elegant effect. Each rail and style is engraved with bold hieroglyphic script, filled in with black pigment, which give the titulary consisting of the five " Great Names " assumed by the king on his accession ; namely, " The Horus-name," " The Nebty-name," " The Golden-Horus-name," the Prenomen and Nomen. The queen's cartouche and her titles are also included on one of the rails. The four square feet upon which the casket stands are shod with silver caps. The interior of this casket is divided into sixteen rectangular compartments, each measuring $4\frac{3}{8}$ by $3\frac{1}{2}$ inches. The compartments were evidently made to receive a similar number of gold or silver vessels for cosmetics. These were all missing—pilfered—and in their places were cast a small rush basket, a stained ivory bowl, two palettes, an ivory and gold burnisher, an ornamental case for writing-reeds, and an empty mirror-case, all of which obviously came from some other box or casket.

The fifth box is of plain whitened wood similar to the third example referred to. Upon this box is a docket in hieratic reading : " *The . . . procession of the bed-chamber.*" Lying on the bottom of the box were a few dried fruits and a beautiful but very fragile ostrich-feather fan of the king (Plate XVII,A). This simple but touching relic is made up of white and dark brown ostrich feathers inserted into a semi-circular piece of ivory, to which the handle of the fan is attached. The handle, also of ivory, takes the form of a papyrus umbel and stem ; it is bent at right angles to increase the movement caused by the turn of the wrist when in use ; it is ornamented with gold collars, and has a lapis lazuli coloured glass knob at the end. Such charming relics seem to elude time ; many civilizations have risen and died away since that fan was deposited in this treasury. Such a rare, but in many ways familiar, object provides a link between us and that tremendous past. It helps us to visualize that the young king must have been very like ourselves.

The sixth casket (Plate xv,A) stood behind the first, near the doorway. It is the smallest among this group ; it is of simple rectangular shape ; it stands on four square legs, and is ornamented with an ivory and ebony marquetry-inlay and ivory veneer, as in the case of the first casket. We found it empty with its lid on the top of the second casket. A hieratic docket written upon it reads : ". . . *of gold in* (?) *the place of the funeral procession.*" The interior of this casket is divided into equal compartments to take four vessels, which, in all probability, explains the lacuna at the beginning of the inscription.

By the dockets written upon some of these caskets, e.g. " *Jewels of gold of the procession made in the bed-chamber of Neb-khepru-Re,*" " *The . . . procession of the bed-chamber,*" ". . . *of gold in* (?) *the place of the funeral procession,*" " *Gold rings belong to the funeral procession,*" and from scenes of funeral processions in private tomb-chapels of the New Empire, we glean that the jewels, etc., in these treasure caskets were regular features in the funerary ceremony.

Our investigations establish the fact that the material missing from these boxes was at least sixty per cent. of the original contents. What was left of the actual jewellery comprises : some ear-rings, a necklace, a number of pectoral ornaments, some bracelets, and a finger-ring. There were also a lid of a small open-work jewelled box, some sceptres, two mirror-cases, the residue of some vestments, and a writing outfit—forty-three pieces in all. The exact amount of jewellery taken is of course impossible to tell, although the remaining parts of some of the stolen ornaments enable us to conjecture that it must have been considerable, but we can tell that two mirrors, at least twenty vessels from two of the caskets, four of which are stated to have been of gold, were stolen.

Apparently, jewellery in ancient Egyptian days had not served and completed its purpose with death, for we find it in all its forms deposited in the tomb for after-life. It becomes apparent that, with those ancients, its purpose was not only in the service of the living, but in that of the gods; it was also made for burial with the dead. In the latter case it is generally recognized by its flimsier character.

In this tomb, jewellery (amuletic and otherwise) had been deposited in large quantities. One hundred and forty-three pieces were placed upon the king's mummy, some pieces were found within the portable pylon of Anubis, and the remainder stored in these and other treasure caskets. The king's mummy, with all the personal and amuletic ornaments upon it, was untouched. But, as we have just seen, the greater mass, probably those of more intrinsic value, had been stolen from the caskets. Thus we have found only a portion of what was originally placed there. Moreover, it is apparent that the " sergeants of the necropolis," who reclosed the tomb after the raid, must have found what was left in extreme disorder; they seemed to have carried out their duty in a careless and perfunctory manner. What was left had evidently been gathered up and put back into the caskets regardless of the original order. We found parts of an ornament in one casket, parts in another, and the whole mass in confusion.

Although probably not forty per cent. remained of what was originally there, from our point of view there was more than enough to enable us to study the skill of the jeweller, as well as the goldsmith's work in the royal workshops of the late Eighteenth Dynasty.

As a prefatory remark, it may be here said that in many ways these New Empire specimens do not exhibit the same perfection of finish as we find in the workmanship of their Middle Kingdom predecessors. There is shown, however, by the Theban jewellers, excellent skill in execution, a marked decorative sense, and much inventiveness in symbolical device. Their craft included that of the lapidary and the glass-cutter, inlaying, chasing, repoussé-work, embossing, twisted gold wire filigree-work, and granulated gold-work. The last craft is a prominent feature in this jewellery, and it comprises a decoration of minute spherical grains of gold, in all probability fused or sweated to the curved or flat gold surfaces of the objects thus treated. In all these arts great ingenuity and mastery of handicraft is exhibited. Many of these ornaments, in fact most of them, are worked *à jour*, upon which various semi-precious stones and polychrome glass were inlaid, either in high or low relief, or quite flat after cloisonné fashion. It must, however, be understood that the term " cloisonné," applied to ancient Egyptian jewellery, may be misleading. It really means that stones and their glass substitutes were cemented into the metal cells or *cloisons*, and that the encrustation was not enamel, as in the case of true cloisonné-work. Enamel was unknown to the ancient Egyptians.

The metals employed were gold, electron, silver and, in a lesser degree, bronze; the natural stones were amethyst, turquoise, lapis lazuli, calcite, carnelian, chalcedony, green felspar, semi-translucent and translucent quartz often backed with pigment for brilliance and imitative effects, serpentine, and an obscure hard olive-green stone not indentified. In addition to these were composite materials such as faience (glazed pottery), hard vitreous paste, semi-translucent and opaque coloured glasses, used in the place of some one or other of the above-mentioned stones. But perhaps the most remarkable material used in the composition of this jewellery was a dark coloured resin, both on ornaments and as beads. Another peculiarity in these ornaments is a brilliant scarlet tinted gold, produced by a method which is at present unknown. This, when overlaid with bright yellow gold ornamentation, such as the granulated gold-work, and in combination with the dark coloured resin, imparted a strange and somewhat barbaric effect.

The theme of the various devices employed in these ornaments has, in great part, some subordinate connexion with the state religion. Of these designs Re, the Sun-god, and Aah (Thoth), the Moon-god, are the nucleus, if not the principal. Re, the sun itself, " Lord of Heaven," " The Sovereign King of all Life," takes many forms in this jewellery, such as Khepre, Horus, Herakhte, and Atum, each being a local representative of some phase of the sun. With the ancient Egyptians, especially at this moment, there was no god of higher standing than Re. They regarded him as the Master of the Universe, who, from his sacred barque in the heavens, governed all things. To speak of God was to think of Re.

Khepre, the scarab, is a transformation of the Sun-god in the form of the famous dung-beetle, who scrupulously constructs the maternal ball provided with a cavity in which the egg will hatch and be nourished. It was in this form that the newly-born sun issued from the "Cavern of Dawn" to begin his diurnal career. On his awakening in the east he enters into the Morning barque to ascend the heavenly vault, when he is identified with Horus, either as a youth or as a Hobby-falcon (*Falco subbuteo*). A prayer refers to Re with these words: "*Beautiful is Thine awakening, O Horus, who voyagest over the sky . . . The fire-child with glittering rays, dispelling darkness and gloom.*" As he triumphantly hovers in mid-air, he is conceived as a great disk with multi-coloured wings ready to pounce upon his foe. During his heavenly course he also takes the shape of Herakhte, either in anthropomorphic form as a falcon-headed man, or as a peregrine falcon (*Falco peregrinus*)—a highly courageous bird of prey that kills its quarry upon the wing. Finally he becomes the old man, Atum, "The Closer of the Day," and enters into the Evening barque, descends behind Manun, the sacred Mountain of the West, into the Underworld to begin again his nocturnal journey through the twelve caverns—the hours of the night. There, we gather from a song, he gives light to the great god Osiris, "The ruler of Eternity." "*Give me light, that I may see thy beauty,*" is also the prayer of the dead.

From such mythological considerations as these, there can be little doubt that Pharaonic jewellery was looked upon as sacred. They may have believed it to have possessed magic powers ; it may be, too, that priestly orders attached to the court had special charge of it. Underlying its themes of design there certainly appears to lurk an ulterior idea. Thus we find these jewels of Tut·ankh·Amen, though it may be made for daily use, designed so as to serve a purpose in the world to come.

But associated with these ornaments there is a problem of some intricacy—how much of it is real and intended for daily use, and how much of it was made solely for sepulchral purpose ? It must be remembered that more than often sepulchral and real jewellery are so closely alike, that the distinction, if any, is far from easy to recognize. In fact, in most cases the only criterion would be flimsiness or evidence of use. There are some examples, however, which are clearly sepulchral. For instance, the eight pectorals discovered in the pylon of Anubis. Three of them are inscribed with funerary spells which have direct relation to the heart and limbs of the deceased, the others bear epithets such as :— " *Osiris, the King, Justified,*" the equivalent to our word " deceased."

The ear-rings seem to have belonged to Tut·ankh·Amen in his earlier youth.

When examining the mummy of Tut·ankh·Amen, it was found that the lobes of his ears were perforated, but among the numerous ornaments that we discovered within his wrappings there was nothing of the nature of an ear-ring. The gold portrait mask that covered his head had also the lobes of the ears pierced, but the holes had been carefully filled in with small disks of thin sheet-gold, suggesting an endeavour to hide the fact. Among the representations of kings upon the Empire monuments, perforations in the lobes of the ears are often marked, but I am not aware of any instance of actual ear-rings being depicted on a king's ears. Osiris is represented wearing collars and bracelets, but never ear-rings. On Arab boys in Egypt ear-rings (*halak*) are often worn up to the age of six and seven years, when they are generally removed and given to the lad's younger brother or sister; in rare cases of an only, or favourite, child they are worn up to the age of twelve to thirteen. Therefore, when taking into consideration the evidence afforded by the king's mummy, his mask, the monuments, and the modern custom which is probably a survival of an earlier practice, it would seem that wearing ear-rings was not customary after the age of manhood. Ear-rings were not an early form of Egyptian ornament. They apparently begin to appear among the inhabitants of the Nile about the commencement of the New Empire, and were probably introduced into Egypt from Asia during the preceding Intermediate Period, under the domination of the Hyksos kings.

There are two types of ear-rings represented here—the rigid and the flexible (Plate xviii). In both cases they were fixed to the ears by means of studs passed through the perforations of the pendulous lobes. It is of interest to note that the solar falcon, Herakhte, represented on one of the pairs of ear-rings, has, for some unaccountable reason, the head of a mallard (*Anas boscas*) in semi-translucent blue glass (Plate xviii,c).

75

The principal and most popular articles of jewellery in ancient Egypt, whether for kings or commoners, were bead-necklaces and broad bead-collars. Many forms of collars and necklaces were prescribed for the funerary equipment. Their popularity as ornaments among all classes of people proved, in this case, to be our loss, for, with the exception of one crude string of alternate dark resin and lapis lazuli beads, they were all taken. They were stolen, probably, not so much on account of their intrinsic value, which cannot have been very great, but on account of their universal popularity. We found beads dropped here and there on the ground from this treasury to the entrance passage of the tomb, particularly at the spot where the thieves had to pass through a small hole, made by them in the masonry that blocked the doorway of the Burial Chamber (Vol. I, p. 181); there we found broken portions of necklaces hanging on the jagged edges of the stones and many beads dispersed in the cracks of the masonry—parts of at least two necklaces and some falcon-headed " shoulder "-pieces from broad bead-collars.

The " pectoral " is a kind of ornament which Egyptian kings wore in great variety, but almost all of them are similar in the following particulars. A breast ornament suspended from the neck either by chains of contiguous ornamental plaques (Plate XIX,A), by strings of beads (Plate XIX,C), by plain gold chains, or by simple twisted linen cords ending in tassels (Plate XIX,B). In the case of the first three forms of suspension, they almost invariably have a " dorsal " ornament which acted not only as a counterbalance at the back of the neck, but as an ornamental fastening; these dorsal ornaments are often made to open and close, and thus they served as the clasp (*see* Plate XIX,A.C.). Many magnificent examples of pectorals were found in the caskets, some complete, others having parts missing. Some might even have been honorific orders; for example, see the pectoral ornament representing " The Birth of the Sun " (Plate XIX,A), which eclipses anything of the kind hitherto discovered.

Bracelets were perhaps the most constant articles of jewellery among all Egyptian classes. Here, unfortunately, we found only three examples (Plate XX,A) left by the thieves. From these specimens it will be seen that they fall into two categories: of solid metal hoop type, with pin-hinges, pin-fastenings, and encrusted with ornament; or of wrist-band type composed of beads arranged by means of " spacers " into a definite pattern, with a centre-ornament and pin-fastenings.

The only finger-ring that we found in these caskets was of somewhat poor type, composed of blue faience mounted with thin electron. The small but beautiful ivory box (Vol. I, Plate LVII) bearing a docket in hieratic on its lid, reading: " *Gold rings belonging to the funeral procession,*" and the massive gold rings tied up in the corner of a scarf (Vol. I, p. 138, Plates XXX, LXVII), that were recovered in the Antechamber during our first season's work, very probably came from here.

Perhaps the most important objects among this collection of jewellery are the insignia of royalty; the two crozier-sceptres and two flagella (Plate XXI,A). The crozier, or kind of pastoral staff, was one of the insignia of Osiris. It was held in the left hand of both the god and the king. It takes the form of a

short staff ending at the top in a crook bent inwards
and outwards, and in this case it is made up of sections
of gold, dark blue glass, and obsidian, upon a bronze
core. It was called "*hekat*" by the ancient Egyptians, and it may be said to have given origin to the
pastoral staff used by cardinals and bishops. Both
the specimens found here bear the cartouches of the
king engraved upon their gold-capped ends. The
flagellum, a kind of whip or scourge commonly known,
especially in the Vulgate, as the "flail," was the
complement to the crozier-sceptre and the second of
the insignia proper of Osiris. It was held both by
the god and by the king in the right hand, and was
called "*nekhekhw.*" It consists of a short handle,
bent at an acute angle at the top, to which are
attached three "swingles" by means of beaded
thongs, in such a manner as to enable them to swing
freely. These two specimens are made in similar
manner to the croziers, save for the swingles which
have wooden cores in place of bronze. The larger
example bears the prenomen and nomen of Tut·ankh·
Amen ; the smaller one bears his Aten name in place
of the Amen name, suggesting that it belonged to the
earlier part of the young king's reign, before he was
converted to the worship of Amen. Its smaller size
is also in keeping with this hypothesis. It becomes
fairly evident that these insignia were but symbols of
authority over the two principal factions in early
times : the Husbandmen and the Shepherds.

With regard to the mirror-cases (Plate xxi,b) and
their mirrors, we have the same tale to record. Their
reflectors were made of solid metal and in consequence
were stolen. Some fragments of the ivory portion
of the handle of one of them were discovered in the

Antechamber, where the thieves broke it off and cast it away. The mirror-case in the form of the symbol of " life " is lined with silver-foil; the second case, in shape symbolizing eternity, is lined with gold-foil; the mirrors were probably made of the corresponding metals.

The simpler whitened wood boxes held objects of the nature of vestments, like official garments, which were taken apparently for the value of their costly adornment. All that was left was a pair of sandals, some much deteriorated linen wraps, and a most interesting bead and gold ceremonial scarf (Plate XX,B) suggesting an early form of a liturgical vestment like the modern stole. It is made up of seven rows of flat disk-shaped blue faience beads which, at intervals, are held in place by gold " spacers." The ends terminate in gold cartouches of Tut·ankh·Amen, " beloved of Ptah " and " beloved of Sokar," and, have fringes of " ankh " symbols. It is curved, so as to fit round the neck and must have been worn scarf-wise.

As previously mentioned (p. 68), the writing-outfit that was found thrown into one of the larger ornamental caskets, must have belonged to one of the other boxes in this room, but it is impossible to say definitely to which of them it came from.

According to the funerary spells, known to us as the " Book of the Dead " (Chap. XCIV), the palette, or the scribe's outfit, was essential for the deceased. They were the implements of Thoth, the god of speech, writing and mathematics, and therefore were considered divine. A large number of funerary palettes, with imitation colours and reeds, obviously for ritualistic purposes, were discovered in the Annexe—

another chamber in this tomb. The palettes and writing-outfit found here, I believe, were actually the private property of the king. One of these palettes is plated with gold (Plate XXII,E) and has its colours and reeds intact. It bears the Aten nomen of the king, who is " beloved of the great god Thoth," showing that it may have dated from the earlier part of the king's reign, and that the god Thoth was accepted during the so-called monotheism of Aten. The second palette, made of solid ivory (Plate XXII,B), with its colours and reeds complete, bears the Amen form of the king's name, " beloved of Atum of Heliopolis," " Thoth," and " Amen-Re," which suggests it belonged to the later part of the reign. The colours, red and black, in both cases show evidence of having been used.

The complement of the palette, the pen-case, or to be more accurate, the reed-holder (Plate XXII,D), is a charming relic of the past, reminding one of the schoolboy of to-day. It takes the form of a column with palm-leaf capital ; its elaborately decorated shaft and drum are hollowed out to receive the reeds, and the abacus, turning on a pivot, acts as the lid. It contained a number of fine reeds.

The palette and the reed-holder illustrate the composite hieroglyphic ideogram *sesh* for " writing," " scribe," and related words, which represents a palette, water-bowl and reed-holder. The ivory bowl (Plate LXVI,A) found in our group, although it is not of the same shape as the vessel depicted in the ideogram, evidently served as the water-bowl. This bowl, turned out of a solid block of ivory, is $6\frac{1}{2}$ inches in diameter and shows the size of tusk that could be procured in those days in the upper reaches of the Nile.

Funerary Equipment

The use of the elegant but curious mallet-like ivory instrument (Plate XXII,C) is not so easily recognized ; however, its gold-capped top suggests that it is a burnisher, for smoothing the rough surfaces of the papyrus paper. It is evident that it belongs to this group, as a similar instrument was found with a scribe's outfit discovered by us some years ago in a Theban tomb.[1] The basket (Plate LXVI,B), made of papyrus-pith, lined with linen, and dedicated to Amen-Re, Herakhte, Ptah, and Sekhmet, also belongs to this outfit. Perhaps an idea of its original contents may be gathered by referring to that far less regal scribe's equipment previously mentioned.

But to return to the palette, the reed-holder and the little burnisher, it is of interest to notice the refinement, and exquisite delicacy which pervade them. They furnish a striking and beautiful instance of simplicity, as well as being mementoes of quaint antiquity which impart the charm of the Dynastic Ages. When one discovered the little basket, one hoped, upon opening it, to find some writing, perhaps a specimen of the boy's calligraphy ; but it was void, like the whole tomb, of any form of document.

However much the deceased was identified with Osiris, it would appear that the dead feared the *corvées* (forced labour) for that deity, who, as king of the dead, would continue to till and irrigate the land and plant corn in the *fields of the blessed*, and would deal with his subjects in that world even as he did when he was their great king and agricultural teacher on this earth.

Hence, to escape future destiny, and to protect

---

[1] *See* Carnarvon and Carter, " Five Years' Explorations at Thebes," pp. 75–77, Plate LXVI.

the deceased from such irksome duties as might be entailed by a *corvée*, we find stored in this room, as well as in the Annexe, large numbers of sepulchral-statuettes called *Shawabti*-figures, representing the king swathed in linen, mummiform. Such figures were originally made of *Shawabti*-wood, whence they derive their name ; and their function, according to the sixth chapter of the " Book of the Dead," was to act as substitutes for the deceased in the Nether World, if he be called upon to perform any fatiguing duties, " *even as a man is bounden, to cultivate the fields, to flood the meadows, or to carry sand of the East to the West.*" Upon the deceased being summoned, these figures are bidden : " *Then speak thou, ' Here am I.' *"

Their implements—the hoe, the pick, the yoke, basket and water-vessel—either depicted upon them, or as copper and faience models (Plate LXVII,A) placed with them, clearly indicate the duty which they were supposed to perform for their deceased lord in the future life. That in this case these figures are effigies of the Osirian king becomes manifest from the names and titles upon them, and, in the finer examples, the attempt at likeness to Tut·ankh· Amen (Plate XXIII).

They were housed in numbers of wooden kiosks resting on sledges (Plate LXVII,B), wherein 413 figures and 1,866 model implements were packed. The vaulted roof (i.e. the lid) of each kiosk was carefully tied down with cord and sealed. The figures themselves were made of wood, wood painted, wood gesso-gilt, wood covered with gesso on linen and painted, quartzite, alabaster (calcite), white, yellow and crystalline limestone, grey and black granite, light, dark blue, violet, and white glazed pottery; some carved in the finest style, others modelled in almost primitive form. In the finer specimens, by their own symbolism is expressed the perfect serenity of death.

Engraved on the soles of the feet of six finely carved wood specimens, are dedications indicating that they were especially made and presented for the funeral by high officials and, no doubt, personal friends of Tut·ankh·Amen. These dedications were :

" Made by the true Servant who is beneficial to his Lord, the King's Scribe, Mîn-nekht, for his Lord, the Osiris, Lord of the Two Lands, Neb·khepru·Re, justified."

" Made by the King's Scribe, the General Mîn-nekht, for his Lord, the Osiris, the King, Neb·khepru·Re, justified."

" The Osiris, the King, Neb·khepru·Re, justified, made by the Servant who makes to live the name of his Lord, the General Mîn-nekht."

" Made by the Servant beloved of his Lord, the General Mîn-nekht, for his Lord, the Osiris, the King, Neb·khepru·Re, justified."

" Made by the Fanbearer on the right hand of the King, . . . Mîn-[nekht], for his Lord, the Osiris, Neb·khepru·Re, justified."

" Made by the Servant who is beneficial to his Lord, Neb·khepru·Re, the Overseer of the Treasury, Mâya."

Such dedications confirm Professors Spiegelberg and Newberry's suggestion that figures of the kind were dedicated by servants of the deceased, who devoted their services to their master both in this life and that beyond the grave.

Mîn-nekht is possibly the same man who excavated the tomb for King Ay in Wadyein, who is mentioned on an unpublished stela at Akhmîm of the reign of Ay, and there are stelæ of the same official in the British Museum and at Berlin. For "the Overseer of the Treasury, Mâya," see further mention later on.

Related to the *Shawabti*-figures and reminiscent of Osiris, is a kind of miniature effigy of the dead king that was found in this room in a small oblong chest (Plate XXIV), carefully padded with linen. Carved of wood, it represents a recumbent figure of the king, mummiform, as the divine prototype, lying on a funeral bier of lion-form. This "Osiride" figure of the king lies stretched out at length upon the bed; his head, covered with the *nemes*-head-dress, bears the royal uræus; his hands, free from the wrappings, grasp the emblems of Osiris—the crozier and flagellum sceptres, now unfortunately missing. On the left side a figure of the *Ba*-bird or "soul" protects the mummy with its left wing; opposite, a figure of a falcon, the (?) *Ka* or "spirit," protects the mummy with its right wing, and they seem to be no less than manifestations of divine protection on the part of the "Soul" and the "Spirit" of the deceased king. Placed with this effigy was a set of miniature implements—a pick, a hoe, a yoke and two baskets, of copper—similar to the equipment found with and belonging to the *Shawabti*-figures.

The dedications engraved upon the bier read: "*Made by the Servant who is beneficial to His Majesty, who seeks what is good and finds what is fine, and does it thoroughly for his Lord, who does [or, makes] excellent things in the Splendid Place, Overseer of Building-*

works in the Place of Eternity, the King's Scribe, Over-seer of the Treasury, Mâya."

" *Made by the Servant who is beneficial to his Lord, who seeks out excellent things in the Place of Eternity, Overseer of Building-works in the West, beloved of his Lord, doing what he [his Lord] says, who does not allow anything to go wrong, whose face is cheerful, when he does it [sic] with loving heart as a thing profit-able to his Lord.*" " *The King's Scribe, beloved of his Lord, Overseer of the Treasury, Mâya.*"

The inscriptions upon the effigy are : " *Words spoken by the justified King Neb·khepru·Re : Descend, my Mother Nût, and spread thyself over me, and cause me to be the Imperishable Stars that are in thee.*" " *In honour with* "—Imseti, Hepy, Anubis who is in the place of embalmment, Anubis, Dua·mutef, Qebeh·snewef, Horus and Osiris.[1]

An interesting and historical point regarding this effigy is that it was made by the Overseer of the Works in the Place of Eternity (i.e. the tomb), Mâya, who, as we have just seen, also dedicated a *Shawabti*-figure to the king. He was in all probability responsible for the excavation of the king's tomb, and, in the eighth year of Hor·em·heb, was com-manded, with " his assistant the Steward of Thebes, Thothmes," to renew the burial of King Thothmes IV, which had suffered in the hands of the tomb-plunderers (Vol. I, p. 54). This must have been some eleven years after the interment of Tut·ankh·Amen, and about the time, it would appear, when his tomb was resealed after the sundry plunderings that it had suffered. It is thus possible that Mâya was also responsible for the resealing of Tut·ankh·

---

[1] For these translations I am indebted to Mr. Battiscombe Gunn.

The Tomb of Tut·ankh·Amen

Amen's tomb, for the seals employed on the tomb of Thothmes IV have a peculiar likeness to those used when Tut·ankh·Amen's tomb was reclosed.

During the reign of Tut·ankh·Amen, Mâya bore the titles: "*Overseer of the Building-works in the Place of Eternity, Overseer of the Building-works in the West, Overseer of the Treasury, the King's Scribe.*" But in the reign of Hor·em·heb we gather that he reached the dignity: "*The Fanbearer on the left of the King, the Leader of the Festival of Amen in Karnak,*" and that he was "*Son of the Doctor Aui, born of the Lady Urt.*"

A plain wooden box of oblong shape, which stood on the north side of the Canopic canopy, had its contents completely cleared by the tomb-plunderers. Its gable-shaped lid had been replaced the wrong way on, and only the packing material in its eight rectangular compartments was left. This material comprised pieces of papyrus reeds, shredded papyrus-pith and, at the bottom of each division, a small bundle of linen matting of long pile. There was not a trace of evidence as to what the original contents were, save that the careful arrangement of the packing suggested that the objects were of fragile nature —possibly glass.

Hitherto the discoveries in this tomb have been little more than a succession of objects, or series of objects, forming a brilliant funerary equipment, but here we come across unlooked-for surprises.

Placed on the top of the kiosks of *Shawabti*-figures (*see* Plate IV) was a small wooden anthropoid coffin, about thirty inches in length, fashioned like a coffin for a noble of the period. It was covered with a lustrous coat of black resin, gilded with bands of formulæ pertaining to the guardian divinities and genii of the dead. It was tied with strips of linen at the neck and ankles, and sealed with the necropolis seal. It contained a second coffin of gesso-gilt wood, ornamented after the fashion of a royal coffin, but neither of these two coffins bore royal emblems, although the formulæ inscribed upon them give the names of Tut·ankh·Amen (Plate xxv,A). The second coffin contained a third small plain wood coffin, and, beside it, a solid gold statuette of Amen·hetep III, rolled up in a separate piece of mummy cloth (Plate xxv,A,B,C). Within this third coffin was a fourth, also made of wood, of anthropoid form, but not more than five inches in length. This last coffin was wrapped in linen, tied at the neck with a band of minute bead-work, sealed at the ankles, and was profusely anointed with unguents (Plate xxv,D), as in the case of the king's burial. It bore the titles and name of Queen Tyi, and, within it, carefully folded in linen, was a plaited lock of her hair.

Such heirlooms as these—a lock of auburn hair of the Great Hereditary Princess, the Great Royal Wife, the Lady of the Two Lands, Tyi, and a statuette of her sovereign husband, Amen·hetep III—are evidence of devotion. They were in all probability pieces of personal property that had been in the family, chattels descending by due succession. Tut·ankh·Amen, the ultimate heir, was the last of that ruling Amen·hetep House; hence these heirlooms were buried with him. The gold statuette (Plate xxv,C), suspended upon a chain ending with tasselled cords, to fasten it at the back of the neck, was a trinket and was treated as such; the lock of hair was human, the remains of a royal personage, for which reason it received the prerogative of a royal burial.

But even more extraordinary were the contents of two miniature anthropoid coffins that were placed, head to foot, in a wooden box (*see* Plate IV) beside the last-mentioned coffins. These were also fashioned in the manner such as would be used for a high personage. They were coated with a black lustrous resin, and ornamented with bands of gilt formulæ pertaining to the tutelary divinities of the dead, but dedicated only to a nameless " Osiris " (i.e. deceased). The coffins were carefully fastened with strips of linen in three places—at the throat, at the centre, and at the ankles, and each fastening was sealed with clay bearing an impression of the necropolis seal. Each coffin contained an inner gilt coffin of similar design (Plate XXVI). In one case there was a small mummy preserved in accordance with burial custom of the Eighteenth Dynasty. It had a gesso-gilt mask (several sizes too large for it) covering its head (Plate XXVI,A). The linen wrappings enveloped a well preserved mummy of a still-born child (Plate LI,A). In the other case (Plate XXVI,B) the inner coffin contained a slightly larger mummy of a child of premature birth (Plate LI,B), also wrapped in the prescribed fashion of the period.

These pathetic remains give much food for thought. With little doubt they were the offspring of Tut·ankh·Amen, and, although there is nothing to tell us emphatically, the probabilities are they were the issue of Ankh·es·en·Amen. Possibly, these *two* premature births were due merely to chance : the outcome of an abnormality on the part of the young queen. However, it must not be forgotten that :

an accident to the expectant mother would have rendered the throne vacant for those eager to step in. But interpretation is the exclusive property of the historian, and as an investigation of this kind calls for methodical, scientific and disinterested treatment, I must therefore refer the reader to Dr. Douglas Derry's valuable report given in Appendix I of this volume.

As I have mentioned, the coffins were placed side by side, head to feet, in a box. It is interesting, however, to know that the toes of the foot of the larger coffin had been hacked off because they prevented the lid of the box from closing properly. We noted a similar occurrence in the case of the king's outer coffin (Vol. II, p. 90). Moreover, another curious fact lies in the absence of a mask over the mummy of the larger child. In the cache discovered by Mr. Theo. M. Davis, wherein remnants from the burial ceremonies of Tut·ankh·Amen were found (Vol. I, pp. 77–78), there was a gesso-gilt mask of similar dimensions and character to that found here on the smaller child. Could it be the one intended for this larger mummy, and that it was omitted owing to its being too small to fit over the head ?

The contents of another box in this group certainly call for description. The box had been sealed in the usual way, but this fastening was broken and its lid left partially open, indicating that it had been ransacked by the robbers. The box was empty save for sixteen small model implements, one of which was found dropped on the floor beside the box. Unexpected surprises are often the fate of an archæologist : these miniature model implements, fixed into hard, dark-grained wooden handles, proved to be of iron (*see* Plate xxvii).

Two of the instruments are lancet-shaped (*a*), two are twisted at the point into graver-form (*c*), two are of chisel type with a slight waist in the shank (*e*), three are shaped like an ordinary chisel (*g*), three others are similar to group (*e*), but have longer handles (*j*), lastly, four comprise fan-shaped chisels set in short, flat handles (*m*). The blades are approximately half a millimetre in thickness, their length and breadth vary from 2·7 to 1·5, and 0·85 to 0·30 centimetres, respectively, and they are coated with the familiar red rust. Mr. A. Lucas, who examined them, adds :

"They have all the appearance of iron coated with oxide ; they are attracted by the magnet and fragments of the corroded surface give the usual chemical reaction for iron. The corrosion may be removed (and in one case was partially removed), by the means of strong nitric acid, leaving a bright surface of metallic iron."

Such objects seem to be out of place among ritualistic material belonging to a funeral cult of a king, nor is it conceivable that so large a chest could have contained only these small implements. Their frail and somewhat flimsy make suggests them to be models and not actual tools for use. And, if such be the case (they were not ritualistic), it throws a totally different light upon their significance in the tomb, as well as their historical value with regard to the use of iron in Egypt during dynastic times. By their being models, their presence here might be on account of the new or unusual metal ; perhaps they were gifts to the king, to record its arrival or discovery in Egypt. In any case, while recognizing their historical importance, a warning at least is necessary, lest we rush into absurd revelations with regard to that metal and its use by the ancient Egyptians.

Although iron ore is fairly plentiful in the eastern desert of Egypt, and in the Sinaitic Peninsula, and although the extraction of copper required greater metallurgical skill, the Egyptians were almost entirely metallurgists of copper and bronze. It is not until this period that we have any real authentic proof of the use of iron by them, and even in this reign probably only as a strange and new metal. Copper and its successor, bronze, are the common metals through the whole of the Egyptian dynastic period, and iron objects are singularly scarce in Egypt even in the succeeding dynasties and foreign dominations.

Based upon the discovery of accidental pieces of iron, it has been claimed that iron was known and used by the Egyptians since the time of the Great Pyramid, as well as in pre-dynastic days. On the other extreme, I have noticed it mentioned that the scarcity of iron among Egyptian antiquities was due to the fact that the relics are in most cases the paraphernalia of tombs, and that iron being considered an impure metal by the ancient Egyptians was never used by them for religious purposes.

Such arguments I believe to be untenable. For, in the first case, it has been my lot to sift the dust of the plundered tombs of Amen·hetep I and Thothmes I, the two tombs of Queen Hat·shep·sût, the tombs of Thothmes IV and Amen·hetep III, and among the numerous fragments of objects, including the smallest beads and minute pieces of copper and bronze discovered in those tombs, I have not found a single trace of iron until the discovery of this tomb, wherein nineteen separate objects in that metal were found. Moreover, while excavating for many years in the Valley of the Kings, I have found in the various strata of dynastic debris numbers of bronze chisel points, that were broken off during use by the masons when they were hewing out the royal hypogæa; but I never found a vestige of iron, much less an iron tool. In the second case, if iron was 'considered impure by the Egyptians, why were iron emblems such as an *Urs* pillow and an Eye-of-Horus, as well as an iron dagger (Vol. II, pp. 109, 135), placed on the hallowed remains of this Pharaoh, Tut·ankh· Amen? As a matter of fact, from his reign onwards, we find special amulets made of that material for the dead. Here, in this tomb, two of the objects were certainly ritualistic, the others possibly being specimens—at least sixteen of them appear to be mere copies of artisan's implements.

Let us for a moment look at all the collections of Egyptian antiquities in Europe, including the outstanding collection in the Cairo Museum where there are over 50,000 specimens of every kind of object, and see what authentic examples there are of iron. It will, I think, suffice to say here that among all that material dating from the pre-dynastic period down to the last Egyptian dynasties—the result of research-work in Egypt for over a century—only twelve to thirteen instances of iron can be recorded, out of which, including this discovery, only about five can be said to be of indisputable dynastic origin. That is about all we have among—I dare not say how many—tens of thousands of Egyptian antiquities.

Surely such facts should point to the real truth. The Egyptians, excepting perhaps on rare occasions, did not deal with iron. They were a very conservative people; they were metallurgists of copper and bronze, and all their wonderful work was done with those metals.

In conclusion, the historical value of these particular specimens is, I think, more from the point of view of the introduction of iron in Egypt, than the actual use of that metal by the Egyptians. They are undoubted proof of the knowledge of iron in Egypt at this period, but not necessarily of its use to any extent in the country; and, I should here add, that with the exception of the king's dagger all the examples of iron in this tomb show distinct crudeness in their workmanship.

To return to the box in which those iron implements were discovered, there is a possible chance that the four *Ankh*-torches and lamps (Vol. I, p. 113, Plate LXXV), that were found on the cheetah-couch[1] in the Antechamber, came from this chest. We have, in several instances, sufficient evidence to prove that metal objects stored in this room were passed into the Antechamber by the robbers, where they evidently examined them, took or discarded them, or broke off parts of them, according to their thievish greed. Those torch-holders and lamps certainly did not appear to be in their proper place; parts of them were missing, and their wooden pedestals, coated with black resin, coincide with blotches of similar black material found on the bottom of the interior of the box. Their dimensions—the height and area they would occupy—agree with the capacity of the box. The gilding upon the torch-holders might

---

[1] I now believe that cheetahs are represented on that couch and not lions as aforesaid.

have been mistaken for gold in an imperfect light, and the deception discovered upon a closer scrutiny in the Antechamber. This, at least, is a conjecture in the absence of any other explanation.

In the north-west corner of this chamber, leant against the wall (Plate IV,A), was the king's bow-case, ornamented with very fine marquetry decoration peculiar to the Eighteenth Dynasty, and particularly so to the reign of Tut·ankh·Amen. As a matter of fact, the decoration of this bow-case covers two provinces of ornament, namely, the relieved and the flat. The relieved ornament is rendered in embossed (thin) sheet-gold, upon a specially prepared under-surface ; the flat ornament, which is the main feature of this bow-case, comprises a marquetry of different kinds of barks, applied strips of tinted leather and gold-foil, with here and there iridescent beetles' wings, presenting exceedingly harmonious colour. It is a kind of decoration which not only vies in effect and quality with painting, but causes admiration for the patient and skilful workmanship of those ancient craftsmen.

On both the *recto* and *verso* of the bow-case (Plate XXVIII,A), the scheme of ornament is symbolic as well as traditional, the principal theme being idealized hunting scenes, in which the king is the central figure. The framework of the case and the borders surrounding its panels are decorated with garland, palmette, and diaper patterns, which include hiero-glyphic script. Towards the tapering ends of the case, which terminate in violet faience heads of cheetahs with gilded manes, are small symbolic scenes wherein the king, represented as a human-headed lion, tramples upon Egypt's alien foes. The central panels, of embossed gold, represent the king in his chariot, hunting with bow and arrow, accompanied by his hounds, depicted running beside or in front of his steeds, barking, or harassing the quarry (Plate xxviii,B). The triangular panels on either side represent, in the finest marquetry work, various fauna—denizens of the desert—stricken by the king's arrows (Plate xxix).

This bow-case evidently belonged to one of the king's hunting chariots that were found dismantled in this room (Plate iv,A), to which it was fastened by means of copper attachments expressly made for the purpose. It contained three neatly made composite bows, now, unfortunately, in a parlous condition, their gelatinous cores at some early period having become viscid, with the result that they leaked out, and dried into a solid black mass.

A critical examination of the zoology displayed in the triangular panels (*see* Plate xxix) is not without interest. The red antelopes with characteristic long face, and high crest for the angulated lyrate horns, with moderately long and hairy tail, are sufficiently distinctive to identify as representing one of the North African species of the hartebeest. The white antelopes with long horns are either the algazel or white oryx (*O. leucoryx*), or possibly, from the straightness of their horns, the white Arabian oryx (*O. beatrix*). The smaller sandy-coloured antelopes, with sub-lyrate horns, are probably the common dorcas gazelle, or a near allied species. They, like the larger antelope already identified, and also the desert hare depicted on the same panels, are notably inhabitants of the open desert districts, such as the scenes seem to represent. The goat-like animal, with long horns which rise from the crest of the head and bend gradually backwards, having ridges on the front surface, and terminating in smooth tips, obviously characterizes a species of ibex (*Capra ? Sinaitica*). Such antelopes inhabit elevated spots, especially the more mountainous districts. Another somewhat incompatible detail is, that hunting in a chariot with bow and arrow implies a daylight sport, yet we find in these scenes the striped hyena, nocturnal in its habits, preferring by day the gloom of caves or the burrows which it occasionally forms. There is also a still more puzzling detail. Some of the ibex are represented as having large and dark blotches—a feature, I believe, unknown among the African, Asiatic, and European species of that animal.

On the Old and Middle Kingdom monuments, both the oryx and the ibex occur domesticated, and they were fattened for the table. Young ibex kids can be brought up on goat's milk, and readily tamed, and, as ibex will propagate with the domestic goat (Cuvier), it is possible that the spotted kind depicted here is the progeny resulting from such a source. If such were the case, it throws a totally different light upon these scenes, and presents a very interesting point with regard to Pharaonic sporting pursuits. For it suggests the idea that they possibly bred and preserved animals for hunting, and that they had special sanctuaries, or enclosures, for the purpose, like the old Persian *pairidaeza*—a park, or enclosure, in which animals were kept. Hunting within kraals or zarebas, in some instances large areas surrounded by netting, is to be found represented among the mural decorations of the ancient Egyptian tombs.

Lastly, with the dismembered parts of two hunting chariots found in this chamber (Plate IV,A), was a whip bearing an inscription: "*The King's-son, Captain of the Troops, Thothmes.*" Who was this royal prince ?—who, to have been "Captain of the Troops" during the reign of Tut·ankh·Amen, could not have been very young. Was he a son of Thothmes IV, or was he a son of Amen·hetep III ? That problem has yet to be solved. If he was a son of Thothmes IV, and was living at the time of Tut·ankh·Amen's burial, he must have reached at least sixty or more years of age; whereas, if he was a son of Amen·hetep III, as one would suspect him to have been, he would not have been more than about thirty-five years of age at the time of Tut·ankh·Amen's death. Circumstantial evidence of this kind should have some bearing upon the possibility of that prince's parentage.

CHAPTER III

THE ANNEXE

(See Vol. I, p. 223)

(A STORE-ROOM)

STRANGE and beautiful objects call for wonder, conjecture and fair words, but are they not all signs of the thought and progress of the age to which they belong ? Facts, too, also give food for reflection.

During the previous two seasons in the Innermost Treasury we found little cause for criticism upon the general arrangement and state of the objects with which we had to deal. In this winter's work, however, we must qualify our account with a grain of question !

In contrast to the comparative order and harmony of the contents of the Innermost Treasury, we find in this last chamber—the Annexe or Store-room—a jumble of every kind of funerary chattels, tumbled any way one upon the other, almost defying description. Bedsteads, chairs, stools, footstools, hassocks, game-boards, baskets of fruits, every kind of alabaster vessel and pottery wine-jars, boxes of funerary figures, toys, shields, bows and arrows, and other missiles, all turned topsy-turvy. Caskets thrown over, their contents spilled ; in fact, everything in confusion.

Doubtless this confusion was the work of plunderers, but in the other chambers there had been a perfunctory attempt to restore order. The responsibility for this utter neglect would, therefore, seem to rest a good deal on the necropolis officials, who, in their task to put to rights the Antechamber, the Burial Chamber and the Innermost Treasury after the robbery, had neglected this little room altogether.

To exaggerate the confusion that existed would be difficult; it was but an illustration of both drama and tragedy. While contemplating its picture of mingled rapacity and destruction, one felt that one could visualize the robbers' hurried scramble for loot—gold and other metals being their natural quarry; everything else they seem to have treated in the most brutal fashion. There was hardly an object that did not bear marks of depredation, and before us—upon one of the larger boxes—were the very foot-prints of the last intruder (Plate xxx,B).

This little store-room was but another witness of the neglect and dishonour that the royal tombs had suffered. Not a monument in the Valley but bears proof of how false and fugitive is the homage of man. All its tombs have been plundered, all have been outraged and dishonoured.

During the last days of November, 1927, we were able to begin this final stage of our investigations. Two days of somewhat strenuous work had to be spent in clearing the way to the little doorway that conducts to this apartment. The southern end of the Antechamber, where its doorway is situated, was then occupied by a number of large roof-sections of the dismantled shrines that had shielded the sarcophagus which, for convenience, were put there during the earlier part of our work in the tomb. These we were obliged to shift to the northern end of the Antechamber, so as to allow sufficient space for access to this store-room as well as for the transport of the material that it contained.

The doorway of this room, only 51 inches high, and 37 inches wide, had been blocked up with rough splinters of limestone and was plastered over on the outside. The plaster, while still wet, had received numerous impressions of four different sepulchral-seals of the king (*see* Vol. I, Plate xiv). When it was discovered, only the upper part of the blocking remained, the thieves having broken through the lower portion. This breach was never mended (*see* Vol. I, Plate xxviii). The devices of the seal·impressions upon the upper part of the blocking read : (1) "*The King of Upper and Lower Egypt, Neb·khepru·Re, who spent his life making images of the gods, that they might give him incense, libation and offerings every day*"; (2) "*Neb·khepru·Re, who made images of Osiris and built his house as in the beginning*"; (3) "*Neb·khepru·Re—Anubis triumphant over the ' Nine Bows'*"; and (4) "*Their Overlord, Anubis, triumphant over the four captive peoples.*"

The deciphering of the very imperfect seal-impressions is mainly, if not wholly, due to the kind assistance rendered by Professor Breasted and Dr. Alan Gardiner. They spent several days studying them under somewhat difficult circumstances during the earlier stages of the discovery.

When the thieves made their incursion, as I have already mentioned, they forced a hole through this sealing of the doorway; and it was through that hole that we made our first inspection of this room (see Vol. I, p. 103 ff.).

The room, comparatively small—14 feet long, 8

feet 6 inches wide, and 8 feet 5 inches high—gave no suggestion of any kind of finish, nor paid any tribute to taste. It is roughly cut out of the bed-rock, and was intended for its purpose—a store-room.

Traces of the dilapidations of time were visible; the rock-cut walls and ceiling were discoloured by damp arising from infrequent saturations.

The history of this little room, although it may have been unfortunate, was nevertheless romantic. There was something bewildering, yet interesting, in the scene which lay before us. The incongruous medley of material, jostled in wanton callousness and mischief, concealed, no doubt, a strange story if it could be disclosed. Our electric lamps threw a mass of light upon its crowded contents, bringing out many an odd feature in strong relief among that accumulation of funerary paraphernalia heaped up to the height of some four or five feet. Our light illumined strange objects lying one upon another and protruding from remote places and corners. Close by, turned upside down, was a large chair like a fald-stool, decorated in the taste of a distant age. Stretching across the room and resting precariously on their sides, were bedsteads of a form such as is used in the regions of the Upper Nile of to-day. Here a vase, and there a tiny figure gazed at one with forlorn expression. There were weapons of various kinds, baskets, pottery and alabaster jars and gaming-boards crushed and mingled with stones that had fallen from the hole that had been forced through the sealed doorway. In a corner opposite, poised high up, as if in a state of indecision, was a broken box bulging with delicate faience vessels, ready to collapse at any moment. In the midst of a miscellany of every kind of chattel and funerary emblem, a cabinet upon slender legs stood almost unscathed. Wedged between boxes and under objects of many shapes, was a boat of alabaster, a lion, and a figure of a bleating ibex. A fan, a sandal, a fragment of a robe, a glove !—keeping odd company with emblems of the living and of the dead. The scene, in fact, seemed almost as if contrived, with theatrical artifice, to produce a state of bewilderment upon the beholder.

When one peers into a chamber arranged and sealed by pious hands of the long past, one is filled with emotion ; it seems as if the very nature of the place and objects hushes the spectator into silent reverence. But here, in this chamber, where nothing but confusion prevailed, the sobering realization of a prodigious task that lay before one took the place of that emotion. One's mind became occupied with the problem, how it could best be dealt with

The method we were finally obliged to adopt, to remove those three-hundred-odd pieces of antiquity, was, to say the least, somewhat prosaic. To begin with, sufficient floor-space had to be made for our feet, and that had to be done as best we could, head downwards, bending over the sill, which was rather more than three feet above the floor-level. Whilst carrying out this uncomfortable operation, every precaution had to be taken lest a hasty movement should cause an avalanche of antiquities precariously piled up and beyond our reach. More than often, to save an object of heavy nature, so situated that the slightest disturbance would cause it to fall, we were obliged to lean over and reach far out, supported by a rope-sling under our arm-pits which was held by three or four men standing in the Antechamber. In that manner, by always removing one by one the uppermost object in reach, we gained ingress and gradually collected the treasures. Each object, or group of objects, had first to be photographed, numbered and recorded, before they were moved (*see* Plate XXXI). It was by means of those records that we were eventually able to reconstruct to a certain degree what had previously occurred in the chamber.

I must confess that my first impression was that the positions of those objects were meaningless, and that there was little or nothing to be learned from such disorder. But as we proceeded in our investigations, and removed them piece by piece, it became evident that many data could be gleaned as to their original order and subsequent chaos. The confusion naturally rendered evidence very difficult to interpret, and it was also disconcerting to find that our deductions, no matter how correct they may have been, could seldom be definitely proven. Nevertheless, careful examination of the facts, such as they were, disclosed one important point, and that point was : that two separate thefts of quite different nature had taken place in that little apartment. The first theft—for gold, silver and bronze—was perpetrated by the famous tomb metal-robbers, who ransacked the four chambers of the tomb for all such portable material. The second robbery was evidently by another class of thief, who sought only the costly oils and unguents contained in the numerous stone vessels. It also became clear that this Annexe was intended for a store-room, like the similar small chambers in other royal tombs of the Eighteenth Dynasty, for housing oils, unguents, wine and food.

But in this case an overflow of other material belonging to the burial equipment had been stacked on the top of its proper contents.

The material that might be termed extraneous was, I believe, put there, not so much for the want of space, but probably owing to the absence of system, when the equipment was being placed in the tomb. For example, it will be remembered that below the Hathor-couch in the Antechamber there was a pile of oviform wooden cases containing a variety of meats (*see* Vol. I, Plate XVIII). Those by rights should have been stored in the Annexe. But owing to some oversight they seem to have been forgotten, and, the doorway of the Annexe having been closed, they had to be put in some convenient place in the Antechamber, which, in natural sequence, was the last room of the tomb to be closed. Also, part of the series of the funerary boats and figures (*shawabtis*), placed in the Innermost Treasury, were found in this Annexe.

From facts gleaned, we may reconstruct more or less the sequence of events that took place : firstly, nearly forty pottery wine-jars were placed on the floor at the northern end of this Annexe ; next to these were added at least thirty-five heavy alabaster vessels containing oils and unguents ; stacked beside them, some even on top, were one hundred and sixteen baskets of fruits ; the remaining space was then used for other furniture—boxes, stools, chairs and bedsteads, etc.—that were piled on top of them. The doorway was then closed and sealed. This manifestly was carried out before any material was placed in the Antechamber, since nothing could have been passed into this Annexe, nor could the doorway have been closed, after the introduction of the material belonging to the Antechamber.

When the metal-robbers made their first incursion, it is evident that they crept under the Thueris-couch in the Antechamber, forced their way through the sealed doorway of the Annexe (*see* Vol. I, Plate XXVIII), ransacked its entire contents for portable metal objects, and were, no doubt, responsible for a great deal of the disorder found in that chamber. Subsequently—it is impossible to say when—a second robbery took place. The objective in this case was the costly oils and unguents contained in the alabaster jars. This last robbery had been carefully thought out. The stone vessels being far too heavy and cumbersome to carry away bodily, the thieves came provided with more convenient receptacles, such as leather bags or water-skins,[1] to take away the spoil. There was not a stopper of a jar that had not been removed, not a jar that had not been emptied. On the interior walls of some of the vessels, that had contained viscous ointments, the finger-marks of those thieves are visible to-day. To get at those heavy stone vessels, the furniture piled on top of them was evidently turned over and thrown helter-skelter from side to side. Thus, by realizing the probable cause, the reader may readily guess the effect.

The knowledge of this second robbery throws light upon a problem that had puzzled us ever since the beginning of the discovery of the tomb. Why, throughout its funerary equipment, had quite insignificant stone vessels been tampered with? Why were some of them left empty lying on the floors of the

---

[1] Some abandoned water-skins were found in the descending entrance passage.

chambers, and others taken out and discarded in the entrance passage ? The greases, or oils, that they once contained had, no doubt, a far greater value in those days than possibly we imagine. It also gives a reason for the tomb having been twice reclosed, as traces on the sealed entrance and inner doorway of the passage signified. I believe also that the odd baskets and simple alabaster jars that were found scattered on the floor of the Antechamber came from the group in this Annexe. They are so obviously of the same class, and were probably taken out for convenience by the thieves. The same argument holds good of the solitary *Shawabti*-figure discovered leaning against the north wall of the Antechamber (*see* Vol. I, p. 120). It surely must have come from one of the broken *Shawabti*-boxes in this last little room—for others like it were found there.

Tradition holds that in burial custom each article belonging to tomb equipment had its prescribed place in the tomb. However, experience has shown that no matter how true the governing conventions may be, seldom have they been strictly carried out. Either the want of forethought with regard to requisite space, or the want of system when placing the elaborate paraphernalia in the tomb-chambers, overcame tradition. We have never found any strict order, we have found only approximate order.

Such were the general facts and impressions gathered during this final part of our investigations in the tomb. How much of the interpretation is absolute fact, how much the embellishment of conjecture, would be very difficult, if not impossible, to prove. It may be said, however, that it is a fair interpretation of what had occurred. If one were to record the numerous memoranda taken down at the time of the actual *déblaiement*, for the purpose of disentangling facts, the reader would be easily lost in the labyrinth of both obscure and conflicting data— the forest would be hidden by its trees. For that reason I have given what I believe to be a fair summary of the whole problem. Nothing can ever change the fact that we have undoubtedly found evidence in this tomb of love and respect mingled with want of order and eventual dishonour. This tomb, though it did not wholly share the fate of its kindred, though mightier mausoleums, was nevertheless robbed—twice robbed—in Pharaonic times, and one might here well repeat Washington Irving's words : " What is the security of a tomb ? " I am also of the belief that both robberies took place within a few years after the burial. Facts such as the transfer of Akh·en·Aten's mummy from its original tomb at El Amarna to its rock-cut cell at Thebes, apparently within the reign of Tut·ankh·Amen ; the renewal of the burial of Thothmes iv, in the eighth year of the reign of Hor·em·heb, after it had been robbed of its treasures, throw considerable light upon the state of affairs in the royal necropolis at that Age. The religious confusion of the State at that time ; the collapse of the Dynasty ; the retention of the throne by the Grand Chamberlain and probable Regent, Ay, who was eventually supplanted by the General Hor·em·heb, were incidents which we may assume helped towards such forms of pillage. It must have been a considerable time before even the conquering Hor·em·heb himself was able to restore order out of the confusion that existed at that period, establish his kingdom and enforce the laws of his State. In any case the evidence afforded by those two burials and by this tomb, prove how the royal tombs suffered even within their own Dynasty.   The wonder is, how it came about that this royal burial, with all its riches, escaped the eventual fate of the twenty-seven others in the Valley.

CHAPTER IV

THE OBJECTS FOUND IN THE ANNEXE

(A STORE-ROOM)

IN the preceding chapter I have endeavoured to describe the state in which we found the Annexe, its impressions upon the spectator, and the incidents, suggested by our observations, which may have occurred after it was originally closed. In the present chapter, I propose to describe the principal antiquities that we were able to salve from the wreckage. It was astonishing how some quite delicate objects had survived almost unscathed, in spite of the ill-treatment that they had suffered. For reasons given presently I shall divide the material into two sections.

At the risk of being tedious I repeat that, apart from the exploits of the robbers, clearly there was a suggestion—one might even say demonstration—of confusion, or want of proper system, when the objects were originally deposited. Consequently, evidence as to the intended uses of the various chambers of the tomb is not absolutely clear; moreover, the tomb itself is not orthodox in plan, and is much contracted. Hence, with reference to the different kinds of funerary equipment, traditionally attributed by the ancient Egyptians to each chamber, much of the evidence gathered still requires sifting and testing. Nevertheless, it may be safely assumed that this

Annexe was merely a store-room intended for provisions, wines, oils and unguents. For this reason,
the objects described in Part I of this chapter may
be termed " extraneous," since possibly they were
not really intended for the room, but were placed
in it for want of space elsewhere. The second group
—Part II—I believe to be the traditional contents
of this store-room, called the Annexe. The nature
of the material seems also to call for this division.

PART I

Extraneous Objects not Traditionally belonging to the Annexe

(A Store-room)

On the top of this mass of material, and stretching
from side to side of the chamber, were three large
bedsteads, resembling in form the modern Sudanese
angarîb. They have wooden frames, a string webbing, at one end foot-panels, and are supported by
fore and hind legs of feline type. One of them, of
not much account, was badly broken ; the second
specimen, of ebony gilt, although of not very fine
work, was in fair condition ; but the third specimen
(Plate XXXII,B), of carved ebony overlaid with stout
sheet-gold, was in almost its original state, save
for warping due to its having rested so long upon
an uneven surface. The proportions of this last
bedstead are perhaps finer than any of the others
found in this tomb. From its characteristics it
was evidently of El Amarna make, the subject of
its ornament being purely floral, namely, garlands
of petals and fruits, bouquets, clumps of papyrus and

red-tipped sedge, chased and embossed upon burnished gold (Plate XXXII,C), and signifying Northern
and Southern Egypt. It is interesting to note how the
strengthening transverse stretchers under its framework are curved, in order to be clear from sagging
of the webbing, when the bedstead was slept upon.

Underneath a mass of every kind of chattel at
the southern end of the room (*see* Plate XXXI), we
found a fourth very interesting folding bedstead,
made expressly for travelling purposes. It is constructed of a light wood painted white, and is of
similar design to the specimens already described, but
it conveniently folds into one third of its size by
means of heavy bronze hinges (Plate XXXII,A).

I shall now turn to the most varied and familiar
articles of domestic furniture : chairs, stools, footstools and a hassock, which were appanages of seig-
neurial right and, in fact, at that period the emblems
of authority.

Wedged topsy-turvy in the south-east corner,
between the wall and one of the bedsteads, was an
elaborate chair, perhaps better named a " faldstool,"
which vies in rank with the so-called secular throne
found in the Antechamber (Vol. I, pp. 117-119,
Plate LXIII). There is nothing to tell us definitely
its use, but its extremely elaborate detail, and its
austere appearance, suggest that it is of an entirely
different order from the rest of the chairs. Indeed,
in character, it seems appropriate only to a " Chair
of State," like the specimen named " the secular
throne," which is far too rich and ornate for any
ordinary house use. In point of fact, it would appear
to have been the king's ecclesiastical throne when
presiding as the highest spiritual authority ; and, in

many ways, it recalls the bishop's chair, or faldstool,
of our cathedrals to-day. It is of faldstool-form, but,
while retaining its folding shape, it had at that early
period already become rigid and acquired a back
(Plate xxxiii).

Its ample, curved seat, fashioned in the sem-
blance of flexible leather, is made of ebony inlaid with
irregular-shaped pieces of ivory, which imitate the
motley markings of a piebald hide. The central portion of the seat, however, is ornamented with a series
of small rectangular panels of ivory, stained to
represent various other hides, including that of the
cheetah. The seat is supported by cross legs of
folding-stool type ; these are carved in ebony and inlaid with ivory in the shape of heads of geese, and
are partially bound with thin sheet-gold. Between
the stretchers and the foot-bars is an openwork gilt-
wood ornament symbolizing the union of the " Two
Kingdoms "—Upper and Lower Egypt—the greater
part of which was wrenched away by the dynastic
tomb-robbers in search for loot.

The upper part of the upright curved back-panel
is overlaid with sheet-gold, and richly inlaid with
faience, glass, and natural stones. Here the decoration incorporates the Aten disk and names, the prenomen and Aten-nomen of the king, and the Nekhebet vulture holding single ostrich-feather fans. Below
this device is a series of inlaid rails and stiles enclosing
ivory and ebony panels inscribed with various designations of the king. Of particular interest are these
inscriptions, for they give both the Aten and the
Amen forms of the king's nomen, and in all cases
the Aten form remains unchallenged. This fald-
stool is thus an important historical document with

regard to the politico-religious vacillations of the reign, for, from the fact that the Aten and the Amen elements occur side by side, it would appear that the young king's return to the older faith of Thebes was gradual in transition and not spontaneous.

At the back, to give rigidity to this folding-stool form of chair, upright laths were fixed to the back-panel, the seat and the back foot-bar. The upper rail and supporting laths are encrusted with designations of the king, which include the Aten form of his name. The back of the back-panel is overlaid with sheet-gold, and upon it, finely embossed, is a large Nekhebet vulture with drooping wings surrounded by various complimentary epithets.

The strengthening framework of this chair, warped by infrequent saturations of humidity which the tomb had suffered, no longer serves its purpose, for its tenons do not now meet their mortised sockets. Thus this relic of authority offered more than one problem in the matter of reparation, even though it were only sufficient to ensure its safe transportation from the tomb to the Cairo Museum. With this chair was found its companion footstool (*see* Plate XXXIII), equally rich in workmanship. It is made of wood, overlaid with violet glazed pottery, and inlaid with ivory, glass, and natural stones. Upon the " tread " are the traditional nine alien foes of Egypt, wrought in gold, ebony, and cedar-wood, arranged so that the king's feet would rest upon Egypt's enemies.

There was something almost humorous, yet pathetic, in the situation of a small white chair (Plate XXXIV) possibly from the royal nursery, high-backed, animal-footed, turned upside-down among such plebeian

I   113

society as oil and wine jars, and hampers of fruits, with which it was obliged to associate. Like its companion stool (Plate LXVIII,B) with gilded ornament between its seat and stretchers, it clung to the bedsteads of the royal household. Jammed down below the door-sill of the chamber, and crushed by heavy stone vessels, was another stool, also painted white, but in this case three-legged and [with semi-circular seat (Plate LXVIII,A). This somewhat ornate specimen has an open carved wood seat representing two lions bound head to tail. The rim is decorated with a spiral pattern. Like its companions just described, the space between the stretchers that brace the framework of the legs is filled in with open-work traditional throne ornament—the " Two Kingdoms " —Upper and Lower Egypt—bound together under the monarchy. In addition to its peculiar shape, it has a particular feature of its own which makes it in some ways unique. Most Egyptian chairs and stools have either the conventional bovine and feline or sometimes duck-headed legs, whereas the legs of this semi-circular stool are of canine form. Although thus fallen into decline and discoloured, these chairs and stools still bear traces of their former environment.

Opposite the doorway, on the top of the material stacked against the west wall, was a rush-work garden-chair. The seat and back were covered, and the sides of the under-framework trimmed, with painted papyrus. The painted decoration on the back consisted of petals of the lotus-corolla, and on the seat the " Nine Bows," i.e. bound Asiatic and African prisoners in elaborate costume. The rush-work (mostly split papyrus stalks) and the papyrus covering, were too far decayed to allow of more than a few fragments being preserved.

There were also several miniature rectangular footstools tucked away in sundry places. These are made of cedar-wood or ebony, one of them combining the two kinds of wood and being embellished with ivory (Plate LXIX,A). Their dimensions seem appropriate only for a child. Of particular interest was a hassock (Plate LXIX,B) such as we might find in use to-day. Unfortunately it bears marks of having seen better days, but sufficient of it remains to show that it doubtless figured in some ceremony. Though of ordinary rush-work, covered with plain linen, it is enriched with complicated and brilliant polychrome bead-work, depicting alien captives bound and prone around a central rosette. This device, a conventional ornament usually associated in ancient Egypt with footstools and mats (cf. Vol. I, p. 119), is encircled with garland patterns, and the sides of the hassock are enclosed in a bead net-work of lace-like appearance. The footstools were obviously for the regal foot ; maybe the hassock was intended for the royal knee.

Lodged in a very precarious position, amidst miscellanea in the centre of the chamber, was a cabinet, standing on four slim legs, and about twenty-three inches in height (Plate XXXV,A). It is one of those quaint pieces of antiquity which has all the peculiar charm of the lighter Egyptian furniture, as well as all the aspects of what it pleases us to call " modern " workmanship. Its rich, dark red cedar-wood panels are quite plain ; its ebony uprights, rails, and stretchers are encrusted with eulogistic titulary and other designations of the king in hieroglyphic script ;

and between the bottom of the cabinet and the stretchers it has an open-work frieze symbolizing " All Life and Good Fortune," made up of a fretwork of alternate gilt and plain ebony emblems. The top folds back on bronze hinges fixed to the top rail of the back of the cabinet. On the top and front panel are gilt knobs, to which a cord and a seal were once attached. If one may judge by the hieratic docket written on the panel of its fellow cabinet (Plate XXXV,B), which was found broken in this chamber, this piece of furniture was probably intended for the fine linen raiments of the king. But its contents had been scattered, or perhaps stolen, and in it we found four very fine head-rests that had evidently been put there after the robbery.

The first of these head-rests (Plate XXXVI,B) is a magnificent example of ivory carving—perhaps the finest piece of Egyptian New Empire symbolical art we have hitherto discovered—and in addition to receiving the tint of age, it is in perfect preservation. The theme of its design seems to be an impression of the official religion, and its subject founded upon one of the early conceptions of the " cosmos," when all things fell into their places. The myth it represents conceives Geb and Nût—the Earth-god and the Sky-goddess—as husband and wife, separated by their father, Shu, the god of Atmosphere. The caryatidal figure, Shu, thrusts himself between earth and sky, and raises the sky-goddess into the heights, together with all the gods hitherto created. Nût, the goddess of the sky, took possession of the gods, counted them, and made them into stars. At the east and west extremities of earth (i.e. the foot of the head-rest) will be noticed the lions of " Yesterday and

The Morrow." They probably symbolize the rising and setting of Re, the Sun-god and progenitor of all beings, mortal and immortal, or it may be that they represent the coming and going of Osiris—the deceased. The figure representing Shu (atmosphere), raising heaven into the heights and the two *arît*—lions of the East and West horizons—are full of dignity. The observer cannot but be sensible of the serenity of this little monument, inspired, it would seem, by a kindly and happy feeling that the king, when at rest, would lay his head in heaven and, perhaps, become a star in the firmament. The second head-rest (Plate XXXVI,A) takes the shape of a miniature folding stool in carved and tinted ivory. Although it is a fine example of craftsmanship, it lacks the supreme dignity of the first piece. Instead, we find in it the love of the grotesque, its main feature being the head (tinted dark green) of the hideous male demon Bes—a household god held in superstitious veneration, who was of dwarf stature, his duty being to amuse the gods with his tambourine and to tend the divine children. The third head-rest (Plate LXX,A) is of rich lapis lazuli blue faience. In this case the æsthetic takes the place of the symbolical, for bold form and rich colour—lapis lazuli blue embellished with gold—is its main feature. In the same manner is fashioned the fourth head-rest (Plate LXX,B), which is wrought out of opaque turquoise-blue glass, with a collar of embossed gold around its stem. These head-rests belong to the ritualistic equipment entailed by Egyptian burial custom. The deceased is given them for his future benefit. The State artificers, while keeping within the limits of the convention, seem to have taken pride in rendering them for their royal master as simple and beautiful as possible. They have no sameness; each piece has some salient feature, which makes it a variety of the traditional *urs*-pillow prescribed by the " Book of the Dead," to " lift up the head of the prostrate One."

Among the series of ornamental caskets, a much ill-treated but wonderful specimen was found at the northern end of the chamber. The lid was thrown in one corner, while the empty casket itself was heaved into another, and its legs and panels damaged by the weight of material heaped upon it. Although its ornamentation comprises an ivory veneer, beautifully carved in relief like an early Greek coin, and stained with simple colours, it has borders of encrusted faience and semi-translucent calcite, and may be placed in the same category as the painted casket discovered in the Antechamber (cf. Vol. I, p. 110 ff., Plates XXI, L–LIV). The central panel of the lid (*see* Frontispiece) is certainly the unsigned work of a master, but, in contradistinction to the warlike scenes upon the painted casket, the motive here is purely domestic. It depicts the young king and queen in a pavilion bedecked with vines and festoons of flowers. The royal couple, wearing floral collarettes and dressed in semi-court attire, face one another; the king, leaning slightly on his staff, accepts from his consort bouquets of papyrus and lotus-blooms; while, in a frieze below, two court maidens gather flowers and the fruit of the mandrake for their charges. Above their Majesties are short inscriptions : " *The Beautiful God, Lord of the Two Lands, Neb·khepru·Re, Tut·ankh·Amen, Prince of the Southern Heliopolis, resembling Re.*" " *The Great-Royal-Wife, Lady of the Two Lands, Ankh·es·en·Amen,*

May she live." The subjects of the side and end panels pertain to the chase, their compositions being friezes of animals, and the king and queen fowling and fishing, much like the scene upon the small shrine that was found in the Antechamber (Vol. II, Plate I). As to the contents of the casket, when deposited in the tomb, we can only make a conjecture (*see* p. 124).

There were also three small chests, which are interesting mementoes of the king's youth. Their damaged parts were scattered here and there, they have bronze staples for suspension, like panniers, and were evidently intended to be used for travelling purposes, strapped either on the back of a beast of burden, or over the shoulders of a slave (Plate LXXI,A). They have a framework of ebony, panels of cedarwood, and are inlaid with ebony and ivory. The dockets written upon their lids tell us that they were : " The linen chests of His Majesty, when he was a youth," and that they contained—I imagine this to be a subsequent docket—incense, gum, antimony, some jars and gold grasshoppers. We found pieces of incense and gum (resin), antimony powder, and small jars of faience, gold, and silver, dispersed on the floor of the chamber, but nothing in the way of gold grasshoppers !

Scarcely any object has such peculiar interest as a box especially made for the king's head-wear (Plate XXXVII), that had been thrown among a lot of wine-jars at the northern end of this room. Its very domestic nature makes it at once appreciated by everyone. It is a legacy from the daily life of the past, and, one might even say, the prototype of the hat-box that is in use to-day. Save for a simple blue and yellow faience and semi-translucent calcite decoration bordering its panels, it is a plain rectangular wooden case, with hinged lid, containing a block-headed support for a cap. The remnants of the young king's cap were found at the bottom of the box. It was made of fine linen, embellished with elaborate beadwork of gold, lapis lazuli, carnelian and green felspar. Unfortunately, the dilapidations of time had caused the textile fabric to decay beyond recovery. There are, however, sufficient traces of its former splendour to enable us to get a record of the order of its beads, and a general idea of the original form of the skull-cap itself. Strangely enough, on the lid was a docket, reading: " What is in it," and mentioning " *Shawabtis* " ! This leads one to believe, that for some reason—possibly for economy—some of the funerary statuettes had been put in it at the time of burial. Or it may be, in this case, that the word has not been properly understood.

Over and above the specimens just described there were seven other broken boxes. With the exception of one chest, they are all of somewhat rough make. Of these I will mention the examples that have a particular interest attached to them. The first (Plate LXXI,B) is a chest of far more solid make than any box we have found in this tomb, and the few remains of its contents throw not a little light upon the pursuits and amusements of a child of the Egyptian New Empire The interior of the chest is fitted with complicated partitions, and with box-shaped drawers that are made to slide one above the other, and each provided with a sliding lid. These fittings had suffered from rough treatment; they had been wrenched open by impatient hands, evidently in search of what valuable material they may have contained. The chest was apparently for knick-knacks and playthings of Tut·ankh·Amen's youth, but, unfortunately, everything in it had been turned topsy-turvy; moreover, we found many of its trinkets strewn on the floor. A few of the things that we were able to recover were : a quantity of bracelets and anklets of ivory, wood, glass and leather; pocket game-boards of ivory; slings for hurling stones; gloves; a " lighter "; some leather archer's " bracers," to protect the left wrist from the blow of the bow-string; mechanical toys; some samples of minerals; and even pigments and paint-pots of the youthful painter. The exterior of this chest is decorated with the names and titles of the king, as well as with dedications to various gods. Its lid opens on heavy bronze hinges; the fastening of the knob upon the lid is so notched on the inside that when the lid was closed and the knob turned, it locked the lid to the box. This contrivance, I believe, is the earliest automatic fastening hitherto known. The chest itself, some $25\frac{1}{2}$ by 13 by $10\frac{1}{2}$ inches in size, stands on four square feet capped with bronze, and, pegged on the centre of its back frame, is a large wooden *ded*-amulet signifying " stability."

The sense of manliness imparted by the possession of implements in connexion with fire, hunting, or fighting, such as an apparatus for making fire (Plate XXXVIII), and slings for hurling stones (Plate LXXII,A), was evidently as pleasing to the youth of those days as to the boy of our era. Those ancient Egyptians knew nothing of the combustible materials like phosphorus and sulphur, which easily take fire when rubbed on any natural or prepared rough surface, nor did they know of agents such as flint and iron with tinder. Their "lighter"—or, method of creating fire—was of a very primitive nature throughout the whole of their history, from the First to the Thirtieth Dynasty. They created fire by rapidly rotating a piece of stick in a round hole in a stationary piece of wood appropriate for the purpose. For this they applied the principle of the bow-drill (*see* Plate XXXVIII), with which they were so familiar. The rotation was effected by means of a bow alternately thrust forwards and backwards, the thong of the bow having been first wound round the stock of the drill in which the fire-stick was fixed. And, in order to steady the drill, the upper end was held in a socket of stone, ivory, or ebony, or sometimes of the kernel of a *Dôm*-nut, which, when cut in halves formed a ready-made drill-head. The round holes in which the fire-stick was rotated were made near the edge of the fire-stock which allowed the spark to have free access to the tinder. In Tut·ankh·Amen's "lighter" the holes prepared for the fire-stick have been treated with resin, to promote friction, and thus facilitate the creation of heat.

Slings of hide for hurling stones, either for hunting purposes or as a weapon of offence, were probably the earliest device known to mankind, by which an increase of force and range was given to the thrower of such missiles. Although we first know of the sling in warfare about the seventh century B.C., it must have been in continual use in Egypt from barbaric times down to the present day, when it is still used by peasant boys employed in scaring birds from ripening cereal crops. Here, in this toy-chest of the fourteenth century B.C., this sling has already advanced. For it is no longer of hide, but of plaited linen thread, neatly made with a pouch, and a loop at the end of one of its cords, to hold it firmly on the little finger, while the second cord is left quite plain for loosing between the thumb and first finger, when dispatching the missile (*see* Plate LXXII,A). Apparently, to acquire accuracy with a sling, not only a proper sized stone should be used, but the loose end of the sling must be released at the appropriate time, to ensure aim and distance. This probably explains the presence of a few smooth pebbles that we found among debris on the floor of this chamber. This type of sling is exactly the same as was used in recent years by the aborigines (Sakai) and the jungle Malays in Malaya.

Among the royal youth's bracelets and anklets there is one of particular historical interest. It is cut out of a solid piece of ivory, and carved round the upper bevel are various animals of the chase. The fauna depicted include the ostrich, hare, ibex, gazelle, and other antelope, and a hound chasing a stallion, showing that even then the domestic horse was allowed to run wild in the *pairidaeza*, much as ponies are given the liberty in our own ancient royal hunting demesne, the New Forest. There were also two pairs of bracelets, in faience, bearing the names of Tut·ankh·Amen's predecessors, Akh·en·Aten and Smenkh·ka·Re.

The little game-boards I shall mention anon, with others of more pretentious kind that were found here.

Another box, crudely made and painted red, is worthy of mention. It was broken and bulging with a large number of delicate vessels of pale-blue faience

(Plate LXXIII,B.C.). We found it poised high up against the wall opposite the doorway, with one of its sides fallen away, but fortunately the protruding vessels were sufficiently wedged together to prevent them from falling out (*see* Plate XXX,A). They were the bane of our work when clearing that part of the room, for any unfortunate movement, before we could reach them, would have caused these vessels to fall and crash down into a hundred pieces. This box seems to have been the fellow to a box discovered in the Antechamber (No. 54), which contained similar vessels but of lapis lazuli blue faience (cf. Vol. I, pp. 116, 174, Plates XVIII, XXXVII). A similar box, without lid, that rested on the top of a lot of baskets in front of the doorway (*see* Plate XXX,B), contained a quantity of miniature light and dark blue faience fore-legs of a bovine animal. In addition, thrown carelessly in, was an odd mixture of things : two crumpled-up gala robes, a pair of gloves, a pair of rush sandals, and a ritualistic turquoise-blue glass palette, which certainly did not seem to belong to the box. The amuletic significance of the faience fore-legs is unknown.

Judging from the experience gleaned from the contents of the boxes found here, and in the Antechamber, the wearing apparel came from the better-class caskets previously mentioned, and the crudely made boxes, when originally deposited in the tomb, had contained faience vases and miscellanea, discovered scattered about this and other chambers.

The two garments, which I have chosen to call gala robes, recall official vestments of the character of priestly apparel, such as the dalmatic worn by deacons and bishops of the Christian Church, or by kings and emperors at coronation. Unfortunately, their condition, or, rather, their preservation, is far from what could be desired. They had been crumpled up and bundled into the box with, as we have just seen, a whole lot of ill-sorted objects. They have also suffered deterioration set up by damp from infrequent saturations that had occurred in the tomb during the long past, but, although they were thus treated and have fallen into decay, they still bear traces of their former beauty. In their pristine state they must have been gorgeous pieces of colour. They take the form of a long loose vestment, having richly ornamented tapestry-woven decoration with fringes on both sides. In addition to this ornamentation, one of them has needlework of palmette pattern, desert flora, and animals, over the broad hem at the bottom (Plate xxxix). The opening for the neck and at the chest are also adorned with woven pattern. One of the vestments, with field quite plain, has narrow sleeves like the tunicle; the other, with the whole field woven with coloured rosettes as well as figures of flowers and cartouches across the chest, has its collar woven in the design of a falcon with outspread wings, and it also has the titulary of the king woven down the front.

I cannot claim to be versed in the history of such garments, but from the fact that I discovered a fragment of a similar robe in the tomb of Thothmes IV, bearing the name of Amen·hetep II, it may be inferred that robes of this kind were customary apparel among the Pharaohs. Perhaps they were worn on special occasions, such as religious rites—solemn consecration or coronation—and that they were symbolical of joy, very much in the manner of the dalmatic placed upon a deacon when the holy order was conferred, whereby the following words are repeated by the acting bishop : " May the Lord clothe thee in the Tunic of Joy and the Garment of Rejoicing." Moreover, these robes may well have had the same origin as the Roman garment, whence the liturgical vestment—the dalmatic—of the Christian Church derives. Vestments of the kind were in use in Egypt during the Egypto-Roman period (first to fourth centuries A.D.), and Professor Newberry has acquired a portion of such a garment, also of woven linen, dating from Arab times (Sultan Beybars, thirteenth century A.D.), which is almost identical in treatment of design with the fragment of the robe of Amen·hetep II of the fourteenth century B.C.

In much better preservation were the pair of gloves (Plate XL), neatly folded, also of tapestry-woven linen. They were possibly intended to go with the robes,[1] and are similarly woven with a brilliant scale-pattern and have a border at the wrist of alternate lotus buds and flowers. These gloves are hemmed with plain linen, and have tape to fasten them round the wrist. Although their fabric was in a better condition than that of the dalmatics, it was nevertheless in a fragile and powdery state, but, thanks to Dr. Alexander Scott's good advice with regard to chemical treatment, both of the dalmatics were recovered from their parlous condition, and one of the gloves successfully unfolded for exhibition.

The remaining boxes of rough workmanship were

[1] A Roman Catholic bishop wears gloves when pontificating—also buskins, tunic and dalmatic under his chasuble.

found empty, and are too dilapidated to claim description.

Among this heterogeneous pile of chattels we found two curious-looking white wood cases. One of them was shaped like an attenuated shrine, about $25\frac{1}{2}$ by $2\frac{1}{4}$ by $1\frac{3}{4}$ inches in dimensions, which apparently once held a heavy metal standard cubit-measure. Naturally, the cubit was taken by the thieves on account of its value in metal, thus robbing us of valuable data as to the true linear measurement employed at that period, which, as far as we are able to estimate, must have been a unit something like 52·310 ms. having 7 palms of ·07472 ms., and 28 digits of ·01868 ms. The other case, from its size, shape and make, was evidently a rough chest for bows, arrows and perhaps other missiles. We found in it a number of different kinds of bows, arrows, clubs and boomerangs in a state of confusion (*see* Plate xxx). The bows and arrows, no doubt, belonged to the case, but it is questionable whether the boomerangs did not come from one of the boxes just mentioned. These weapons I will describe later with others which had been scattered about the room.

A most remarkable and fragile object wrought of alabaster (calcite) stood upon the floor almost unscathed. It takes the form of a boat floating in an ornamental tank (*see* Plates xli, lxxiv). I have named it a " centre-piece " (for what else could it be ?) carved of semi-translucent alabaster, engraved and painted with chaplets of fruit and flowers, as if to figure at a banquet or celebration of some kind. There is something extremely fanciful about it, as well as interesting, for is it not but another glimpse into the faded past breaking forth from the gloom of the tomb? The piece is not on a grand scale, being but 27 inches in height and 28 inches over all in length. The details, coloured with pigment and embellished with gold, are sufficiently clear in Mr. Burton's photographs as to need but little description. The tank is designed as a pedestal, of pylon form, resting on four cylindrical feet, and it is hollowed out for water and flowers, with an island in the centre to support the alabaster boat. The boat represents a carvel-built barque, with round bottom, both the stem and stern rising in a curved line and terminating with the head of an ibex. Amidships is a canopy, supported by four ornate papyrus columns, which shields what appears to be an open sarcophagus; the whole representing perhaps a funeral barque for the celestial journey of the " Good God," the king. Facing forward, on the fore-deck, is a charming little figure of a nude girl, squatting and holding a lotus flower to her breast (Plate LXXIV,A). At the helm, steering the boat, is a puny slave (Plate LXXIV,B), which brings to mind the dwarfs at the helms of the Phœnician ships mentioned by Herodotus. This little achondroplasic female dwarf, with inward-turned feet, is as rare an example of fine art as it is in medical research. A mere glance at the photograph suffices to realize how beautifully, and how accurately, both of these female figures and the ibex heads have been rendered by the court stone-carver who wrought this fascinating ornament. With regard to the medical aspects of the dwarf steering the boat, Lord Moynihan, the famous surgeon, says :

" Achondroplasia is a congenital disease of uncertain causation. It produces a deformity so distinctive that the appearance of one man afflicted with it is characteristic of all. The achondroplasic is of low stature, of sturdy muscular and bony development. The head is large; the forehead, broad and high, bulges so much over the face as to leave a deep impression at the base of the nose; the nostrils are large and open; the lower jaw assertive. The body is long in proportion to the limbs; there is a deep incurvation in the lumbar spine, making the abdomen protrude, the arms and legs are short; the feet and hands are broad and strong. Typical examples are portrayed by artists from the earliest days. In Ancient Egypt the god Bes, 'the amuser and instructor of children,' and the god Ptah (Pataikos, son of Ptah); show all the attributes. In the Bayeux tapestry the dwarf Turold is a fairly good example. Velazquez painted many, for the achondroplasic was often a Court dwarf. Nicholas Pertusato is a flawless specimen. Artists have often shown the dwarf in charge of animals. Tiepolo shows achondroplasics with dogs and with a lion. Earliest of all, the mural sculptures at Saqqareh show an achondroplasic leading a monkey almost as large as himself. The achondroplasic seen on this alabaster boat is a female; the disease is far commoner in males. The feet are turned inwards so much that progression must have meant the lifting of one foot over the other."

Lord Moyniham also adds: " the characteristic bodily and facial deformities are here exquisitely portrayed."

Nothing, hitherto, has been found to enlighten us as to the true nature of this little monument. It is a relic of times gone by; of customs and manners with which ours have no affinity. Should, by chance, it belong to the series of model funerary barques, such as were found in the Innermost Treasury (*see* pp. 56–61), of which many damaged and wooden examples were also found here, then it belongs to the purely ritualistic objects pertaining to burial custom. But, so far as can be ascertained, it seems to be purely fanciful, much like the little silver boat discovered among the Kames and Aah·hetep jewellery, and for that reason I am inclined to believe it to be a palace ornament and not really intended for funerary purpose.

An interesting piece that excites attention is a silver vase, about $5\frac{1}{4}$ inches in height, in the form of a pomegranate fruit (Plate LXXIII,A). The vase was probably dropped or forgotten by the tomb-plunderers. The silver being slightly auriferous, the metal is preserved in almost pristine condition. Its bowl is chased with a band of cornflowers and olive leaves ; the shoulders and neck with chaplets of lily and poppy petals. In aspect, the vase is modern enough to resemble the work of the silversmiths of the Queen Anne period, and, did we not know its provenance, none of us would dare to date it as belonging to the fourteenth century B.C.

Gaming-boxes for diversion with their playing-pieces were scattered far and wide about this room, even some of their parts were discovered in the Ante-chamber, where they had been thrown during the dynastic plundering. They are of three different sizes—large, medium, and quite small—for the house, and of portable form for the pocket (*see* Plates XLII, LXXV). The latter size, small and made of plain ivory, came from the knick-knack chest previously described (p. 121). Their presence in the tomb is apparently justified by some mythical precedent, which the deceased hoped to enjoy in the life to come (cf. " The Book of the Dead," Ch. XVII) ; however, the smaller specimens, at least, seem to be chattels of an everyday pastime. The largest and most important of the games, $21\frac{1}{2}$ by 11 by 7 inches over all, rests upon a neat black ebony stand, made like a small stool upon a sledge, having the " cushions " and claws of the feet embellished with gold (Plate LXXV,B).

The game-board—or rather, by its being purely a game of hazard, the gaming-board—is also of ebony, but faced top and bottom with ivory, and of a rectangular oblong shape. The medium sized specimen, about 11 by $3\frac{1}{2}$ by $2\frac{1}{4}$ inches in measurement, of ivory veneered upon a basic wood body, is beautifully decorated with stained carving and gilt borders (Plate XLII,B). Each game is divided into thirty equal squares, so arranged as to form ten by three —the three rows of ten squares being on its long axis. To each game there were ten playing-pieces, like pawns in chess, coloured black and white (i.e. five for each opponent), which were played by complicated chances denoted either by a kind of dice in the form of knuckle-bones, or small black and white throwing sticks (Plate LXXV,A), to which different values were attached according to the manner of their fall. The contest was obviously an early form of, and allied to, the modern game called " *El-Tab-el-Seega*," played almost universally in the Near East —a game of chance, from which one has been able to solve the principles of these ancient forerunners. They were played according to set rules but were decided by luck, and although they involved little or no skill they, nevertheless, afforded an amusing and an exciting pastime. I would even go so far as to say that the modern games of skill, like " *Seega*," or draughts, and chess, were in all probabilities evolved from games of hazard, such as we find from time to time in ancient Egyptian tombs, and so well represented in this burial.

These gaming-boards or boxes have almost invariably each two forms of the game : the three by ten on the top, already mentioned, and three by four with an approach of eight squares on the bottom (*see* Plate XLII). The playing-pieces (pawns) of the large household example are missing; they were probably of gold and silver and consequently stolen in ancient times. The smaller specimens, by being of ivory, had little value in the eyes of the metal-robbers; thus we find them complete.

There were also a number of ostrich-feather fans recalling the flabella still used at a papal procession in Rome, such as was witnessed in the Eucharistic procession of His Holiness the Pope, in July, 1929. These fans, like the pontifical flabella, were carried by grooms-in-waiting in Pharaonic processions, or were held beside the throne, and appear always on either side of the king or immediately behind him. In fact the title, " Fan-bearer on the Right (or Left) side of His Majesty," was considered one of the highest offices among the court officials. The long-handled fans of this form, from their early Egyptian name *shwt*, meaning " shadow," or " shade," were probably intended more for sunshades than for agitating air, although, manifestly, they could have been, and were, used for both purposes. Curiously enough, the hieroglyphic ideogram or determinative of the Egyptian word *tay khw* " Fan-bearer," shows a similar stock to these examples, but without the flabellate top and with only one ostrich-feather, of which form we find no example in this tomb. Another name for the flabellate type was *sryt*, meaning " (Military) Standard," which indicates a further use of this very decorative, and what I believe to be the royal form, of the flabellum.

Unfortunately, the ostrich-feathers of all these fans were so decayed that only in a few cases the shafts of the feathers remained, and they again were in such a bad condition that it was almost impossible to preserve them. However, there were sufficient remains to show us that the flabellate or palmate tops of the fan-stocks, into which the quills were fixed, once held 48 feathers (i.e. 24 on each side), and that the shafts of the feathers had been stripped of their " vanes " for a short distance above the quills (*see* Plate XLIII,D), so that a portion of the bare shafts was visible, like radii, and, thus, must have resembled the radiating framework (" sticks ") of the modern folding fan.

The fan-stocks vary from 2 feet to 4 feet in length, and they comprise a " capitulum " in the shape of a papyrus-umbel and calices, a stem, and, at the lower end, a knob in the form of an inverted papyrus umbel or corolla of the lotus. They are made of solid ivory, carved, stained and gilt (Plate XLIII,B) ; or of ebony veneered with decorative barks (Plate XLIII,C), and more rarely of engraved and embossed sheet-gold upon a wooden core (Plate XLIII,A). The gold specimen bears the prenomen, nomen, and epithets of Akh·en·Aten, as well as the two cartouche-names of Aten, the sun-disk. The stained ivory specimen is a gorgeous piece of ornamental carving.

Another very interesting and unique specimen discovered in this Annexe, was one of the king's sceptres (Plate XLIV). It is difficult to comprehend why such a sacred object should be in a store-room of this kind, and not where one would have expected it to be, among similar insignia in the Innermost Treasury. The only explanation that I can suggest is that, either the plunderers cast it there owing to some misgivings in stealing it, or that it belonged to a complete outfit which included the garments pertaining to religious ceremonies, such as rites in which the king controlled the principal parts, that were originally deposited in one of the ornate caskets found in this chamber. The latter hypothesis is perhaps the most probable, since an adze of bronze inlaid with gold (its gold blade had been wrenched off by the dynastic thieves), that belonged to ceremonies performed in front of the dead, was also discovered among the objects strewn all over the floor. This kind of sceptre is known under several names, and, I believe, always as a staff, or symbol, of authority. As a *kherp*-sceptre it was used in connexion with offerings; this is indicated by the embossed decoration on one side of the " blade " (Plate XLIV,B). It is about 21 inches in length, and is made of thick sheet-gold beaten on to a wooden core. It is embossed and inlaid; the tip, " capitulum," and the two ends of the shaft are richly embellished with (Egyptian) cloisonné-work. The gold and blue faience inscription reads : " *The Beautiful God, beloved, dazzling of face like the Aten when it shines, The Son of Amen, Tut·ankh·Amen*," which is of interest, as it suggests a compromise between the Aten and Amen creeds.

The deceased was looked upon as a man in after death as in life; a king was a " Good God " both in life and in the hereafter; the illustrious of the long past were considered as divinities, and these divinities were called " Great Gods," and they and their divine families were worshipped—in fact the second life was considered but a continuation of the first. Thus we find movable possessions, such as household chattels, sceptres, fans, walking-sticks, staves, weapons and the like of daily use deposited in the tomb—they were burial offerings to the deceased, still living in memory, and through them may be visualized a picture of an ancient world.

The young Tut·ankh·Amen must have been an amateur collector of walking-sticks and staves, for here, as in the Antechamber and the Burial Chamber, we found a great number. They were, no doubt, in part, of ritualistic significance, but many of them have evidently seen daily use. There are many types : long staves with knobbed and forked tops and ferruled ends, crooked sticks, and curved sticks for killing snakes. Some beautifully mounted with gold and silver, others decorated with a marquetry of barks, or with the polished wood left plain.

The collection of weapons of offence that were found in this chamber comprise clubs, single-sticks, falchions, bows and arrows, boomerangs and throwsticks for fowling and warfare. For defence there were real and ceremonial shields, and a cuirass.

The most primitive of the weapons are naturally the clubs, and, from the fact that they figure largely among the levies from the surrounding barbarian countries, they would appear to be more characteristic of foreigners than of the Egyptians. There were many, and they were mostly found in the rough white bow-box mentioned on p. 127. Most of them are falciform (i.e. gradually curved over at the thick end, and in shape like a sickle), with either the suggestion of a knob at the end, or with flattened blade cut like a sickle, the concave edge being the sharper (Plate LXXVI,A). Another, but rarer, type is of cudgel form much like an elongated policeman's truncheon with a pronounced knob on the end of the handle (Plate

LXXVI,B). They are all of a heavy, dark polished wood, and some have the grip covered with a bark resembling that of the silver-birch tree.

The single-sticks (Plate XLV,A) are the first hitherto discovered in Egypt. They had been thrown on the floor of the chamber in the south-west corner. Six of them were about 25 inches in length, and one 37 inches. They consist of a round stick, thicker at one end than the other, and were used apparently as a weapon of attack and defence. In contradistinction to the modern European form of singlestick, the thicker end of the weapon formed the point and it was ferruled with metal, and the thinner end was the handle, which suggests they descended from the club. Protection for the hand was furnished by a leather " guard," somewhat like the " baskethilt," which was made rigid by means of wire, and adorned with an open gold-work " guard." These had been wrenched off, but parts of them were found scattered on the floor. The handle, or " grip," was packed with leather bound with string, in order to prevent repercussion from passing to the hand. It will be noticed from the illustration (Plate XLV,A) that they all have wire loops for (?) suspension ; three have a sheet-gold mounting for a long distance up the grip ; one has bark decoration ; and three— quite plain sticks—have their natural bark intact.

From scenes upon the Egyptian monuments depicting a kind of " cudgel-play," or " single-sticking," guards, cuts and parries appear to have formed at least part of the play, but a short stick bound to the left forearm, like a splint, was also used to ward off strokes not parried with the single-stick, and it obviously served as an auxiliary guard against the adversary's blows. No trace of this sort of auxiliary guard was found here.

In many ways two bronze falchions (Plate XLV, B and c) are unique : a large and heavy example found with the single-sticks, and a much smaller and lighter one discovered among other miscellanea on the floor.

The smaller falchion (16 in. long) was probably made for the king when a child; the larger and heavier weapon ($23\frac{1}{2}$ in. long) was designed for the time when he reached adolescence. In both cases the blade, shaft, and handle-plate are cast in one piece; the handle-plate being fitted with side plates of ebony. The large weapon seems more fitted for a " crushing " than for a " cutting " blow, its convex edge being only partially developed, which places it hardly a step in advance of the sickle-shaped clubs first described; the blade of the smaller specimen, however, has more of a knife edge. That the larger weapon must have inflicted a severe wound is evident from its great weight, due to the thickness of the back, viz. 0·65 of an inch.

These falchions seem peculiar to the New Empire, i.e. the Eighteenth to Twentieth Egyptian Dynasties, and judging from the sickle-shaped determinative of the hieroglyphic name, it was called *khepesh*. According to Sir Gardner Wilkinson ("Manners and Customs of the Ancient Egyptians," Vol. I, p. 213) " . . . the resemblance of its form and name to the *kopis* of the Greeks, suggests that the people of Argos, an Egyptian colony, by whom it was principally adopted, originally derived that weapon from the falchion of Egypt." It may also be a prototype of the Oriental curved sword, the scimitar, which usually broadens towards the point, but is also falciform.

The bows and arrows were very numerous, of great variety, of a high standard of proficiency, and, to be in keeping with the dignity and rank of the owner, most of them were finely ornamented.

Although among the bows there is an absence of uniformity in any of the following groups, each bow having more or less a peculiarity of its own, they may, however, be grouped into three separate classes : (*a*) the " Self-bow," made of a single stave of self wood, without decoration ; (*b*) the " Self-bow," made of two staves (one for each limb) of self wood, joined at the centre, and the whole length bound with bark ; (*c*) the compound-bow, having the whole length of the stave made of several strips of horn or wood glued together, the " belly " filled in with a gelatinous substance, the whole length bound with bark and minutely decorated. The barks employed to bind and decorate the bows resemble, at least in colour, the cherry and the silver birch, but neither the woods nor barks employed have yet been identified. The few self-bows of single staves are only 27 inches in length ; the self-bows made in two staves are some 29 inches in length, but one of them is only 14 inches. The compound-bows are by far the most numerous, and they range from 44 to 49 inches. Needless to mention, in each case the centre of the bow is stiff and resisting ; the two limbs taper gradually to the " horns " to which the " string " is fitted, but in the case of the single stave self-bows the horn is absent ; the string was fixed by means of a few turns round the end of the limbs. In every case where the " string " of a bow was preserved, it was found to be made of four-strand twisted gut.

It seems that the main difference between the

138

self-bow, which is by far the earliest in Egypt, and the compound-bow (of the New Empire, and probably of a foreign origin), is that the self-bow is more sensitive, and its work mostly done during the last few inches of the pull, while the compound-bow pulls evenly throughout. The different types and sizes of the bows, as in the case of the arrows, were, no doubt, intended for different purposes, like our fire-arms and ammunition : the military rifle, the sporting rifle and gun of various weights and bores, and the pistol.

Among 278 arrows found, there were some sixteen different classes varying in detail and in size (*see* Plate XLVI). These arrows in general comprise : a shaft of reed " footed "—i.e. a piece of hard wood tanged to the reed shaft, to which the " pile " is attached ; a " pile," or point, of bronze, ivory or wood, of different shapes, tanged to the foot, or of glass (in place of flint) chisel-shape, cemented to the end of the foot ; the feathers ; and a tanged " nock," or notch, of hard wood, or ivory. Some of the arrows are three-fletched (feathered), but most of them are four-fletched. They are all " footed " arrows, and with few exceptions of slightly " chested " pattern, i.e. the footed shaft tapers slightly from the beginning of the foot to the pile. The exception was a group of 13 four-fletched " self " arrows of " parallel " pattern. In that case the shaft and foot are of the same thickness from neck to pile, and are made of one piece of wood.

These arrows vary from 36 to 10 inches in length ; one of them is only 6 inches (note the very small bow previously mentioned). The piles vary in type according to their purpose—for warfare and for the chase, for piercing, lacerating or stunning the victim.

Several batches of arrows and also some bows were found in different places in the chamber, but the greater mass of them was discovered in the large white bow-box (p. 127).

The excellence of these bows and arrows make it manifest that at this period of the Egyptian New Empire, the bowyers and fletchers were adepts in their craft. The bows are of somewhat short make, even for people like the Egyptians who were of low stature, but that may be due, in this case, to the youthfulness of the king, as the weight of the bow and the length of the arrow should be adapted to the strength of the archer.

There is every reason to believe that amongst the greater peoples of ancient history, the Egyptians were probably the first and the most famous of archers, relying on the bow as their principal weapon in war and in the chase. As a weapon of the chase the bow was, in its various forms, employed even more than in war. However, it must have had immense military value. The possessor of the bow and arrow could bring down the fleetest of animals and could defend himself against his enemy. The rapidity of consecutive shots is said to average up to four to five a minute. A searching rain of arrows would certainly be a formidable thing to march against. The Egyptians used the bow and arrow in chariots, whence they seemed to have shot equally well as on foot, and for defence against arrows both shields and cuirasses of leather were employed.

In their present state of preservation it is impossible to tell the weight (i.e. the pull) of the bows.

They probably had a range of something like 150 to 250 yards. The penetrating power of the self-bows and a class of " footed " arrows belonging to the Egyptian Middle Kingdom, is well illustrated in a discovery made by Mr. H. E. Winlock of a soldier's tomb at Thebes, which contained some sixty men slain in battle (Bulletin of Metropolitan Museum of Art; *The Egyptian Expedition*, 1925–27; pub. Feb. 1928; p. 12 ff., Figs. 17, 20 and 21). The dried remains of the partially mummified bodies of those men show numbers of arrow wounds such as would have been received from a height. Some had parts of the arrows actually sticking in them. Several of those arrows, coming apparently from above, struck the men at the base of the neck and penetrated the chest; another which entered the upper arm passed down the whole length of the forearm to the wrist, and one of the men, hit in the back under the shoulder blade, had his heart transfixed by an arrow which projected some eight inches in front of his chest. The range at which those wounds were inflicted is of course unknown, neither is there any record of the type of bow used by the enemy, but, as far as our knowledge goes, only the self-bow was known and used in Egypt at that period. The fragments of the arrows found in the bodies of the men show them to have been of the " chested " pattern, " footed " with ebony, and having blunt ends without " piles."

The self-bow, among the commodities brought from the Land of Punt—a country somewhere on the East Coast of Africa, north of the Equator, like Abyssinia or Somaliland—clearly shows whence they came.

Another form of missile-weapon was the boomerang, of which a great number were found here —both real, and for ritualistic purpose. The real boomerangs were in the bow-box (p. 127).

Boomerangs and throw-sticks were used in Egypt from the earliest to the last dynasties. The boomerang was certainly used for fowling; the throw-stick probably in warfare. Both kinds are represented in this collection. Of the first type among this lot —boomerangs proper—the return and the non-return kinds are recognizable, even though the general form of both weapons is much the same, i.e. curved in sickle-shape, or two straight arms at an angle, the main, or rather the essential, difference being the skew (twist) of the arms, which are exactly opposed in the two kinds. The non-return weapon was apparently thrown like the return type, its reverse twist or skew helping it to travel a greater distance than the ordinary throw-sticks.

Our specimens of boomerangs are made of a hard wood which I am unable to recognize; they are either painted with a polychrome pattern, or bound in part with a bark resembling that of the birch tree (Plates LXXVI, LXXVII). The ritualistic specimens are of carved ivory, mounted with gold caps at the ends.

The throw-sticks here are either of fantastic form (*see* Plate LXXVII,A) or of simple curved shape made of a hard wood. Those made of ebony with ends of gilt are probably ritualistic, like the example made of gilt-wood capped with faience, or those solely made of faience.

For defence there were eight shields : four possibly for real use, and four of ceremonial purpose. Two of the real shields are of light wood covered with hide of an antelope, and have the cartouches of the king blazoned in their centres; the other two, also of light wood and with similar bearings, are covered with skin of the north African cheetah (Plate XLVII,B); the hair and markings on the hides are still in fair condition. These shields have a maximum measurement of 29 by 20½ inches. The ceremonial shields (Plate XLVII,A,C) are slightly larger; they are wood open-work and gilt. They are heraldic in design, and two have devices representing the king as a lion trampling on Egypt's foes of human form, or as a warrior with falchion smiting foes in the form of lion; and two represent him enthroned in this life and in the hereafter respectively.

Another form of defensive armour was a crumpled-up leather cuirass that had been thrown into a box. This was made up of scales of thick tinted leather worked on to a linen basis, or lining, in the form of a close-fitting bodice without sleeves. It was unfortunately too far decayed for preservation.

Among other objects of purely ritualistic significance that were found in this chamber, I should mention: sickles for reaping in the Elysian Fields; various amuletic bronze, wood and stone implements; amulets of stone, faience and gold; wood, stone, and glass palettes; a large part of the set of wooden miniature funerary boats described in Chapter II, p. 56 ff., and a large quantity of *Shawabti*-figures in kiosks belonging to the series placed in the Treasury, mentioned on p. 81 ff.

PART II

THE CONTENTS PROPER OF THE ANNEXE

(A STORE-ROOM)

The oils, fats, unguents and wines, fruits and foodstuffs were, I believe, the contents proper of this Annexe.

The oils and unctuous materials were stored in thirty-four alabaster (calcite) vessels and one of serpentine, which are remarkable for their diversified shapes and sizes. The ten [1] alabaster jars of similar kind found lying on the floor in the Antechamber, emptied and abandoned, in all probability came from this hoard in the Annexe. With rare exception the lids and stoppers of all these vessels had been forcibly removed, thrown aside, and their contents poured out and stolen, leaving but a small amount of residue in each vessel. On the inner walls of some of the vessels that contained viscous substances, the finger-marks of the predatory hand that scooped out the precious material are as clear to-day as when the theft was perpetrated (see p. 103). Many of the vessels were undoubtedly older than the burial of the king. Some of them have their inscriptions carefully erased; others actually bear ancestral names that carry back to the reign of Thothmes III, and some of them show traces of long use, old breakages, and repairs; in fact, they appear to have contained family oils from famous presses, fats and unguents of matured kind, dating back as far as some eighty-five years before Tut·ankh·Amen.

[1] This does not include the four highly ornamental examples, which were *in situ* in the Antechamber (Vol. I, Plate XXII).

The Objects Found in the Annexe

To transgress for a moment from the main subject, these ancestral amphoræ throw light upon some of the objects found in the preceding Eighteenth Dynasty royal tombs. Among the very fragmentary remains of their funerary equipment the presence of older objects has always been a puzzle, and it has been thought that they might be accidental. However, as we find sundry objects bearing the names of predecessors among those much plundered and broken funerary equipments, and similar example in this discovery, does it not show that the inclusion of ancestral material was not only customary, but had some reason ? There is one other point. As the majority of alabaster vessels have been discovered in tombs—in fact, seldom is an important tomb found without the presence of such jars—it might seem that they were made for sepulchral use only. There can, however, be little doubt that they served their particular purpose in daily life, although perhaps not so much as the ordinary pottery vessels, they being more expensive, heavy, and easily shattered. Their special use was for oils and unctuous material, while pottery vessels were restricted principally to wine, beer, water and the like. The stone vessels made expressly for the tomb are more likely to be recognized among the very ornate examples, which by being of elaborate design were rendered, in the utilitarian sense, of little practical use.

These stone vessels range from seven to twenty-six and a half inches in height, and have a capacity from about 2·75 to 14 litres, showing that at least 350 litres of oils, fats, and other unctuous materials were stored in this room for the king. Two of the vessels bearing the names of Thothmes III have their actual capacities marked upon them, namely, 14½ and 16¾ *hîns* respectively. As the *hîn* at that period was about 460 c.cs., they probably contained 6·67 and 7·70 litres of some matured unctuous material. A pair of vases bearing the cartouches of Amen·hetep III have the Amen nomen of the king erased and altered to his prenomen. This shows that the two vases were in use during Akh·en·Aten's reign. Another interesting point is that a vase bearing a carefully erased inscription, faintly shows the previous existence of the prenomen and nomen of two kings upon it, possibly those of Amen·hetep III and Amen·hetep IV, in which case we have indication of a co-regency of those two Pharaohs (*see* p. 3 ff.).

Plates XLVIII, XLIX, LXXVIII and LXXIX show some of the more characteristic types of these jars. The largest vessel of all is the amphora, designed after the shape of the pottery wine-jars (Plate LXXVIII,A). Another amphora, resting on its original " tazza," or circular support, stands 26 inches high (Plate LXXVIII,B). At the bottom of this vessel a small quantity of its oil was left by the thieves; beneath the hardened crust the oil has remained viscid to the present day. Among the more remarkable vessels the following examples call for mention. A vase in the form of a mythical lion (Plate XLVIII), standing upright in an aggressive attitude, quaintly heraldic like a " lion gardant "; his right fore-paw is clawing at the air in noble rage, while his left rests upon a symbol *sa*, meaning " protection," and fitted on to the crown of the head of the lion is the " neckpiece " of the vase in the form of a coronated lotus flower. The decoration of this lion-vase is incised and filled in with pigments; the tongue and the teeth are of ivory. Another vase represents a bleating ibex, rendered realistically (Plate XLIX,B). A third vase takes the form of a crater upon a " tazza "-stand ; it is finely carved with fluted ornament, incised inscription, coloured with pigment (Plate LXXIX,A). A fourth vase, also of crater form, is embellished with an elaborate open-work envelope of semi-translucent calcite (Plate XLIX,A). The workmanship of these vessels is fairly equal in quality. In designing them, the stone-carver gave free play to his fancy, borrowing forms of flowers and animals for their shapes. Some may be heavy and clumsy, while others are distinguished by their elegance and diversity of form. Especially interesting are a pair of attenuated vases with slender necks and pointed bowls : they are ornamented round their necks with simulacra of floral garlands, made of polychrome faience, embedded in the surface of the stone (Plate LXXIX,B).

The pottery wine-jars (amphoræ), three dozen in number, have an historical interest (Plate L). Naturally the wines they contained had dried up long ago, but each of the jars bears a docket, written in hieratic, which gives the date, place and vintage of the wine. From these dockets we learn that the choice wines of the royal cellars came from the Aten, Amen, and Tut·ankh·Amen domains situated in the Delta—some at Kantareh on the east, but mostly on the west branch of the River Nile. We also learn from these dockets that by far the larger quantity of wine came from the Aten Domain, and dates from the IIIrd to the XXIst years, thus showing that the Aten estates were maintained for at least twenty-one years. The wine next in quantity came from the domain of Tut·ankh·Amen, and it is dated as late as the ixth year, viz.: "*Year* 9, *Wine of the House-of-tut·ankh·Amen from the Western River*," followed by the name of the Chief Vintner. This indicates that the king must have been married to the Crown Princess Ankh·es·en·pa·Aten, and was enthroned at the tender age of nine years, for the balance of evidence afforded by his mummy shows him to have been about eighteen when he died. The smallest quantity of wine came from the domain of Amen, and is dated "year 1," which suggests that the reversion to the worship of the capital god Amen may have taken place late in Tut·ankh·Amen's reign.

From the seals upon the wine-jars we gather some knowledge as to the system practised by the ancient Egyptians when bottling, or, as it may be better described, storing wines. Apparently, when the first fermentation was completed, the young wine was transferred to pottery jars, which were closed and sealed by means of a rush bung completely covered over with a clay or mud capsule that enveloped the whole of the mouth and neck of the jar (*see* Plate L,A). While these immense capsules were still soft, they were impressed with the device of the domain to which the wine belonged. The second fermentation thus took place in the jars, and in order to allow the carbonic acid formed during the process of the secondary fermentation to escape, a small hole was made at the top of the capsules. These small holes were then closed with clay or mud, and were impressed with a smaller device of the domain, made expressly for the purpose (*see* Plate L,B). In all probability the interior of the jars was smeared over with a thin coat of resinous material to counteract the porous nature of the pottery; the broken specimens show a distinct black coating on their inner surfaces.

Although many of the wine-jars were broken, there was no evidence of the wine having been stolen. The breakage that occurred is more likely to have been the result of the rough handling by the thieves, when removing and stealing the contents of the adjacent stone vessels previously mentioned.

About a dozen of the wine-jars were of Syrian form—having an oviform bowl, long slender neck, overlapping lip, and one handle (*see* Plate L,C). Being of fragile make, these were mostly broken. Not one of this type bore any docket, but the clay capsules bore an impression of a similar device to the other wines, so one presumes that the wine contained was of Egyptian and not of foreign produce.

Stacked on top of the stone vessels and the pottery wine-jars were 116 baskets, or even more, if the baskets of similar make that were found discarded on the floor of the Antechamber be included. They contained foodstuffs—mostly sundry fruits and seeds, including the mandrake, *nabakh*, grapes, dates, melon seeds, and *dôm*-nuts. The baskets, round, oval, and of bottle shape, vary from 4 inches to 18 inches in their larger diameter (*see* Plate LXXX). They show by their symmetry the natural aptitude of the expert workman. The " strokes " employed in their construction appear to be precisely the same as those used to-day by the native basket-makers. Some of the smaller and finer weaved examples are adorned with patterns formed by interweaving stained with natural grasses. The coarser specimens are made of fibre " skeins " from the fruit-bearing stalks of the date-palm, bound with fronds of the *dôm*-palm, or, as in some cases, the date-palm, which were in all probability first soaked in water to render them both leathery and pliable. The bottle-shaped baskets (Plate LXXX,B) contained dried grapes. On certain festivals the modern Egyptians still take similar baskets of fruits to the tombs of their deceased relatives.

CHAPTER V

The Main Cause of Deterioration and Chemical Changes among the Objects in the Tomb

BEFORE concluding this account of the discovery, it would not be out of place to say a few words concerning the state in which we found the objects in the tomb, and to suggest the main cause of much of their deterioration.

The existence in the past of damp in the tomb is a subject that needs consideration, although it has been treated summarily in the previous volumes.

From every point of view it was a thousand pities that this tomb should have suffered from infrequent moisture filtering through the fissures in the limestone rock in which it was cut. This moisture saturated the air of its chambers, and caused a humid atmosphere to exist therein for what must have been considerable intermittent periods. It not only nourished a fungoid growth, and caused a peculiar pink film to be deposited everywhere, but it destroyed practically all the leather-work by melting it into a black viscid mass. It also caused extensive warping to take place among the varied woods used in the construction of many of the objects. It dissolved all adhesive material such as glue, so that the component parts of many of the articles fell apart. It also resulted in much deterioration of the textiles—an irreparable loss, for among them were rare garments and the like made of tapestry-woven linen fabric as well as of needlework.

Indeed it was this moisture that has necessitated the ten winter-seasons' work (1922 to 1932) that we have devoted to the removal of the funerary equipment from the tomb, for it was obviously necessary first to render it fit for transport, and then for exhibition. Had not this " first aid " been applied with care, not one-tenth of the many hundreds of objects would ever have reached the Cairo Museum in any reasonable form of condition. In some instances the condition of an article necessitated treatment before it could be touched—although at first sight it looked almost fresh, by experiment, the least stress put thereto, showed that it was wellnigh perished. Thus by steady application, aided by kind help and good advice, and at the price of tedium, many a problem was solved, and I am proud to record that not one quarter per cent. of those diverse and beautiful objects was lost. The Earl of Crawford and Balcarres, in his Presidential address to the Society of Antiquaries (July, 1929), rightly said : " the archæologist must be very scrupulous not to destroy—indeed, his province is to re-create—nor should he neglect artistic quality."

Now, in addition to the periods when those objects were exposed to an intensely humid atmosphere, there must also have been long intervals when they were exposed to drought, thus they were subjected to infrequent conditions of expansion and contraction.

When one realizes the disastrous effects of diurnal temperature variations in the open desert, causing the breaking-up of all superficial layers of rocks, the

breaking away of scarp-faces and even the splitting of huge flint boulders, one is not surprised at the extent of damage caused by infrequent changes from damp to drought such as seem to have occurred in this tomb. The more so, when one knows how much of its equipment was constructed of a number of diverse materials : for example, a chest made of an inferior basic wood overlaid with a superior veneer of ivory, ebony and gold ; or a chair or chariot made of several woods and leather and inlaid with different substances such as metals, natural stones, glass and ivory ; or the great protective shrines built of an oak and coniferous wood, covered with gesso, and overlaid with thin sheet-gold. In fact, it is extraordinary, considering their diverse materials and antiquity, how such objects resisted as much as they did so many opposed expanding and contracting tensions. The length of the periods of damp after saturation must have been considerable within those sealed rock-bound chambers, where the prevailing temperature was about 84° Fahrenheit (29° Centigrade).

In order to have some idea of the primary source of water that affected those chambers, the past and present frequency of rainfall in the region of the Valley of the Tombs of the Kings must naturally be considered.

Although the climatic conditions in Pharaonic times were doubtless more or less the same as they are now, we must not forget to take into account the possibility of a greater quantity of morass that existed in the Nile Valley in those ancient days, attracting a greater amount of humidity, if not actual rainfall. The fauna and flora as displayed by the dynastic

monuments indicate the probability of such a condition.[1] However, contrary to the Eastern desert, where almost yearly torrents pour down its ravines, the Western (Libyan) desert, especially in the Theban regions, is indeed rainless to a remarkable degree. The normal preservation of its antiquities as well as sundry inscriptions (graffiti) upon its bare rock faces are in themselves testimony of the past and present climatic conditions.

Years may pass without any appreciable rain falling. During my own experience, covering a period of more than thirty-five years in the neighbourhood of Thebes, I am only able to record four really heavy rainfalls : one in the spring of 1898 ; one during the late autumn of 1900 ; and two quite close together during the autumn (October and November) of 1916.

Notable features of these rain-storms are their comparatively small area and their abrupt border-line. Though they are of short duration—a few hours only—and generally accompanied by powerful electrical manifestation, the downpour within the storm-area is tremendous. It will fill up valleys and turn them into seething rivers. In a few moments

---

[1] The rainfall in Egypt must have been far greater in prehistoric times than in our era. Palæolithic implements that are found distributed over the higher desert terraces bordering the Nile Valley almost certainly prove that semi-desert conditions existed during their epoch. From that time Egypt, or let us say north-east Africa, appears to have gradually reached its present state of dryness. Egypt as we know her is probably not more than ten to fifteen thousand years old. Her alluvial muds are about thirty to thirty-five feet thick. The rate of those deposits appear to have been from three to four inches per hundred years, and they, in all probability, first began when the tributary Blue Nile broke into the White Nile, bringing with it the Abyssinian alluvium. Before then it was the White Nile that brought tropical forms of African life to the Delta, and its progress north to the Mediterranean was undoubtedly marked by swamps, flooded areas and lakes. (*See* Meinertzhagen, " Nicoll's Birds of Egypt," Vol. I, Chap. I, 1930.)

a ravine may be foaming with innumerable cascades carrying rocks down to its boulder-strewn bed. Yet in a very short space of time the scene changes back to its normal arid aspect. The water has rushed down to the Nile Valley, the scoured beds of the stream being the sole evidence remaining of these short but destructive floods of water.

These temporary downpours of water, called by the Egyptians " *El Seil* " (pl. " *El Sayal* "), seem to occur in the Theban district (west bank) on an average at about ten years' interval, but in a particular valley or locality, owing to the comparatively small area of these downpours, it is obvious, by the laws of chance, that the intervals may be much longer.

Any record of an individual valley is of course unknown. It might, however, be calculated by careful examination of a section of the detrital materials forming the bed of a valley, like that of the Tombs of the Kings, where we have a certain amount of knowledge as to dates, by counting the consecutive strata of wind-blown and water deposits accumulated since dynastic times.

During my experience the actual necropolis of the Valley of the Kings has suffered only one of these great downpours, and that was in the winter season 1900–1901. However, there is not a ravine in that region, large or small, which has not been at some time subject to these sudden streams of water.

Needless to mention, it may occur that a ravine suddenly becomes a seething river of rushing water without a drop of rain having fallen in its immediate locality—a phenomenon brought about by a torrential rain-storm far back on the plateau above, whence part, or all, of the water drains into a ravine and

rushes down in full force until it finds its level. I have myself been witness of such an occurrence, which is perhaps worthy of notice. About 4 p.m. on November 1, 1916, the Great Northern Ravine—north and collateral with the Valley of the Kings and confluent at the mouth—suddenly became a great torrent. This was due to a very heavy rainstorm that had taken place on the desert plateau, some fifteen miles north-west, earlier in the afternoon. It is perhaps also of interest to observe the results of that torrent. Before the rush of water had taken place no living plants were visible on the floor of that great ravine. By January the amount of growth of various flowering desert-plants that carpeted the stream-bed was remarkable. Unfortunately my ignorance of botany prevented my recording their species. The plants—some very fragrant—attracted a number of parent moths, notably of the family of *Sphingidæ*,[1] where they deposited their eggs. By the middle of February the larvæ in their last stages were feeding upon the plants ; at the end of March the newly-hatched imago was present. However, only a few of the hardier specimens among the desert plants survived the hot summer months, and by the end of the following spring all had practically disappeared, save their dried scrub.

Now the growth of such vegetation in those arid ravines after a torrent, suggests that the intervals of drought are not longer than the germinating life of the seeds. And this brings to mind another notable fact. There are no signs whatsoever of desert plants having been present in the main Valley of the Kings,

---

[1] *Hippotion* (*Chaerocampa*) *celerio*—the Silver Striped Hawk, and *Deilephila* (*Hyles*) *euphorbiæ*—the Spurge Hawk.

nor in its smaller tributary branches. This absence
of the usual plant growth after rainfall is so remarkable that it calls for reflection. It might be inferred
that the intervals between the torrents occurring in
the Valley of the Kings have been, at least in the
later years, longer than the germinating life of seeds
of desert plants, but when one takes into consideration
the very narrow barrier dividing this valley from the
Great Northern Ravine, such an inference seems
untenable, and there must be other causes. It may
be due to the actual situation of the valley, for the
part of the plateau immediately above the head of
the Valley of the Kings is limited in extent and
comparatively isolated ; consequently the chance of
storm-water draining into it is less. The same
argument might apply to seeds of plants, whereas
the neighbouring valleys are fed from the greater
plateau.

Howbeit, the primary source of infrequent water
in these valleys is, I think, fairly explained.

Now as to the probable cause of those intermittent saturations reaching the chambers of Tut·
ankh·Amen's tomb, which are cut deep down in the
heart of the bed-rock—the lower Eocene limestone.
At first sight it would not be unreasonable before
closer study is made to suppose that the damps were
due to the low and almost central situation of the
tomb in the trough of the Valley, where debacles of
water from sudden torrential rain-storms would
percolate, ooze through the bed-rock, and permeate
with moisture the atmosphere in the chamber of
the tomb. However, although the first part of the
inference may seem to be logical, it proved not to be
the case.

Although it is a fact that the eastern side of the trough of the Valley had been considerably affected by water from such a source, in dynastic times, on the western side, where Tut·ankh·Amen's tomb is situated, there was not a trace of past water to any harmful extent. During our excavations in the area abutting the front of the tomb (prior to its discovery), the ground and sundry antiquities were found to be in a perfect state of preservation. In fact, it was astonishing to see the freshness of the antiquities— letters and sketches in black ink upon splinters of limestone, and other refuse of the dynastic workmen —that were found there. Moreover, there were no signs of moisture having been present in the rubbish-filling of the descending rock-cut stairway, nor any sign of past damp on the sealed door, nor in the rubble filling the sloping passage of the tomb, where, had water been present, it would have immediately percolated through. The surfaces of the walls, ceiling and floor of the descending passage were also unaffected by damp. The presence of moisture in the past was only visible in the chambers themselves, and there it was very evident—a bad omen that augured ill when we breached the lower sealed doorway and entered the Antechamber. However, nothing could have been freer from moisture than the air in those chambers, when we first entered.

From the above facts it becomes evident that the source of moisture was not from the trough of the Valley, and since the only evidence of past damps was in the chambers themselves, the natural surmise is that it found its way in from above, from the sides, or from the back of the small foot-hill under which the tomb is cut ; or, although this is far less likely,

that it originated from sources within the chambers themselves.

So far as damps from sources within the chambers are concerned, there can be little doubt that to some extent moisture had been enclosed in the tomb at the time of burial. Moisture, such as might have been present in fresh plaster upon the walls, or in the mortar used when plastering over the outer faces of the sealed doorways, or moisture present in fresh fruits, wine and various other provisions among the funerary equipment. But dampness of that kind would only cause local trouble, and could not possibly account for the extent of humidity that had so obviously existed from time to time throughout those chambers. The Innermost Treasury contained nothing among its equipment that could give out moisture to any appreciable extent, whereas it was affected just as much as the adjoining chambers. Moreover, conditions such as moisture issuing from the equipment were common to all important dynastic burials, and we know that many of the royal tombs in this necropolis had a far greater amount of moisture enclosed within them, at the time of burial, than this tomb. Large porous pottery water-jars (*zeers*) filled with water, slaughtered bullocks, wines and fruits, etc., were placed in their store-rooms, and the plastering of the walls and ceilings of their burial chambers, as well as their sealed doors, was the common practice. Yet damage from humidity, arising from such a source, was negligible among their equipment.

Although the past humidity was general, the four chambers in this tomb having alike suffered, yet in detail there were certain exceptions. The western ends of the four great shrines that shielded the sarcophagus were in a worse condition than the front (eastern) ends ; the linen pall between the outermost and second shrine was in worse condition at its western than its eastern end ; it was also noticeable that many objects coming from near the west walls had suffered rather more than those on the east side. A further feature from the point of view of harm caused by humidity was that the objects in the Annexe had suffered most. Moreover, minute particles of bronze from masons' chisels that adhered to the limestone surface of the walls of the Annexe were much oxidized, whereas bronze articles among the equipment were affected far less. All such facts, in the writer's mind, point towards the source of trouble coming through the rock from somewhere on the farther (inner) side of the tomb, and, as limestone rock is permeable to moisture, the clue seems to be at the place where sufficient water had collected in the past, to percolate through and have effect.

It is an established fact that water from downpours over the sun-parched ground of these arid ravines does not sink in more than a few centimetres ; it at once forms torrents and flows away to the point of lowest level, which may be many miles distant. The ground is thus little affected except where water is trapped by some hindrance, forms pools, and hence seepage begins.

The foot-hill under which the tomb is cut, rises obliquely from the trough of the Valley to the height of some 70 feet, whence it abuts the scarp of the Valley. The greatest descending slope of the foot-hill is immediately above our tomb, and here the vast hypogeum of Rameses VI is excavated. The tomb of Rameses VI shows no signs whatsoever of the presence of past moisture, neither have I been able to trace any sufficiently harmful source of water on the southern side of the foot-hill that would have had effect on Tut·ankh·Amen's tomb. But the inner-most chambers of the tomb of Hor·em·heb cut transversely through the foot-hill, and situated be-hind, far below, Tut·ankh·Amen's chambers, show considerable injury from expansions and contraction brought about by the presence of humidity followed by drought, whereas the entrance and forepart of that tomb (situated on the south side of the foot-hill) is in quite good condition. Those inner and low-lying chambers of Hor·em·heb's tomb seem to localize the problem, and give us, if not the actual clue, strong pointers as to whence came all the moisture. For, if water found its way through the rock to the depth of Hor·em·heb's sepulchre, why should it not percolate into our tomb ? Our attention and inquiry is thus directed towards the back of the northern side of the foot-hill, or, in other words, to the local-ity above the chambers affected in Hor·em·heb's sepulchre.

An inspection of that region of the country reveals two converging dry water-courses which had been fed during spates by corresponding water-falls over the scarp-face above. These water-courses have, in times gone by, considerably affected that area. They commence by being wide apart, but they converge and become confluent in front of the entrance of the tomb of Mer·en·ptah, whence they formed a cascade and poured into a deep tributary channel (now filled in with detritus) that joins the main trough of the Valley opposite the tomb of Rameses ix.

During our excavations in search of Tut·ankh·

Amen's tomb on the northern part of the lap of the foot-hill, we discovered that a water-course on that side had been dammed in the Nineteenth Dynasty with the stone-chips (debris) thrown out by workmen employed in making the vast rock-cut hypogeum of Mer·en·ptah, with the result that water during spates had been arrested, formed a pool, and flooded Mer·en·ptah's tomb. The spates at some early date must have been considerable, for the debris and detrital material in that region were cemented together by water-action into a mass almost as hard as the superficial limestone itself. Obviously a considerable amount of water had pocketed there; the tomb of Mer·en·ptah was completely flooded, and thus formed a kind of cistern above the inner chambers of Hor·em·heb's tomb.

Fissures of various degrees in size are abundant in the lower Eocene limestone, and especially so in this foot-hill. Some of these fissures are so regular in formation that, to the inexperienced eye, they appear of artificial origin. The fissures traversing the area in question were, I believe, the means of water having percolated down to the heart of the foot-hill. More than probable they have direct connexion with the fissures that exist in the rock of those low-lying inner chambers of Hor·em·heb, as well as having relation with the fissures in the ceilings, walls and floors of Tut·ankh·Amen's tomb. The lips, or rather the edges, of the cracks in the rock of those chambers are water-stained. I am thus persuaded that they are the responsible agents of moisture from above reaching and saturating those underground chambers. Incidentally, the somewhat careless procedure, or want of forethought, on the part of Mer·en·ptah's workmen, was the eventual cause of the total ruin of his own tomb, and of the partial injury to the sepulchral chambers of Hor·em·heb, and was responsible for the deterioration that took place in the sepulchre of Tut·ankh·Amen. Had those dynastic workmen taken more care, and left a free passage for water to get away during spates, the magnificent hypogea of Hor·em·heb and Mer·en·ptah, and the beautiful paraphernalia of Tut·ankh·Amen, would have been in a far more perfect state of preservation to-day. Indeed, but for this ancient oversight, our work instead of taking ten years, might have been finished in one or two.

Another interesting subject peculiar to the tomb of Tut·ankh·Amen, and one which has been a puzzle throughout our work, was the existence of a pink film (soluble in warm water) deposited over all exposed surfaces within the chambers—the ceilings, floors, walls and objects—a phenomenon so peculiar to the discovery that it appears to be part result of the humidity already discussed. This deposit prevailed everywhere; it varied in density as well as in colour—pink to a bright red—in accordance with conditions, but where an object or material covered another, or where an object stood against and protected a part of any surface, the deposit, if not absent, was of a far lighter density, causing either behind or below the object a faintly indicated impression.[1]

---

[1] Lately I witnessed a very interesting demonstration of a somewhat similar effect. My magazine, wherein masses of materials were stored, was set on fire by thieves to cover a theft they had perpetrated. They set fire to a heap of hemp sacks and large rolls of brown paper that were stored in the magazine (an ancient Egyptian rock-cut tomb chamber closed by a heavy modern wooden door). The fire was detected, from smoke issuing from the cracks of the door, within about an hour of ignition ; in fact, in time to prevent any great harm being done, further than charring the sacks and brown

If, as has been suggested, the coloration came from the rock through influence of water, then why is it absent on the rock surfaces that were shielded by objects ?

Although damp affected the tomb of Hor·em·heb, and many other tombs cut in the lower Eocene limestone in other parts of the necropolis, there is no trace in them of the pink deposit that so palpably prevailed here. Those tombs were found almost entirely void of their equipment ; Tut·ankh·Amen's tomb had practically the whole of its funerary equipment intact. This leads me to believe that the humid atmosphere created by those infrequent saturations caused chemical changes to take place among certain materials pertaining to the equipment—especially the leathers and glues—which by process of evaporation deposited and formed this pink film over everything. There must have been periods when, due to condensation, a moist vapour steamed from every article comprising the equipment, and those chambers were like some infernal chemist's shop.

paper which had only smouldered owing to insufficient air in the chamber. Having extinguished the fire and removed the charred sacking and paper, I found, upon inspection, a light amber brown sticky (? resinous) deposit from the smoke all over the walls, ceiling and floor of the chamber, as well as on all the exposed materials stored therein : an effect, except for the colour and nature of the film, exactly as met with in the tomb of Tut·ankh·Amen.

APPENDICES

APPENDIX I

REPORT UPON THE TWO HUMAN FŒTUSES DISCOVERED IN THE TOMB OF TUT·ANKH·AMEN

By Douglas E. Derry, M.B., Ch.B.,
Professor of Anatomy, Egyptian University

(A) The body of a prematurely-born child, probably female.

The length from the vertex of the head to the heels is 25·75 cm.

The body had been carefully wrapped in linen, but this had been removed by Howard Carter. There is no abdominal incision and no indication as to how the body was preserved.

The skin is of a greyish colour, very shrunken and brittle, and the clavicles, ribs and costal cartilages are all plainly seen through it. On the limbs it has become pressed into folds owing to the loss by desiccation of the natural fullness produced by the underlying tissues, and here also the bones of the hands are clearly defined.

The limbs are fully extended, and the hands are resting on the front of the thighs.

There is no sign of either eyebrows or eyelashes. The eyelids are nearly closed and the small aperture between the lids which now exists is almost certainly a secondary result due to retraction of the lids owing to shrinkage of the parts in drying.

On the head are visible many fine whitish hairs of a silky appearance, probably the remains of lanugo.

A portion of the umbilical cord is present and measures 21 mm. in length. The umbilicus is still at a low level.

Allowing for the general shrinkage of the body, it is estimated from the length of the fœtus, the absence of eyebrows and eyelashes and the state of the eyelids, that the intra-uterine age of the child when born could not have exceeded five months.

(B) **This child, probably a girl, whose length from vertex to heels is 36·1 cm., is also of premature birth.**

The skin is of much the same colour and in the same condition as that of the younger fœtus. The linen wrappings, which are in a very fragile state, are still partially attached to the child.

The limbs are fully extended, but in this case the hands are placed beside the thighs in the position of pronation.

The scalp is free from hair except for some very fine downy-looking hairs in the occipital region, but most of the hair has probably come away with the bandages. The eyebrows are distinct and a few eyelashes remain.

The eyes are wide open and the orbital cavity contains only the shrunken eye-ball with no packing.

On opening the head through the anterior fontanelle the cranial cavity was found filled with linen, apparently impregnated with some saline material. The linen had been inserted through the nose. A wire passed through the right nostril appeared in the cranial cavity as seen through the fontanelle.

Umbilicus. There is no sign of the umbilical cord, but the appearance of the navel, which is not retracted, suggests that the cord had been removed by cutting it off close to the abdominal wall and that it had not dried up as it would had the child lived.

The abdominal wall has been opened by an incision 18 mm. in length on the left side immediately above the inguinal ligament and parallel with it. The opening was closed with a sealing of resin. The abdominal cavity is stuffed with linen impregnated with some saline material.

The nails appear to be fully grown, but allowing for the shrinkage of the soft tissues it is possible that they were not fully developed.

The maximum length of the head is 84·0 mm. and the width 73·0 mm.

The length of the fœtus and its apparent development would make it to have been about seven months at the time of birth.

APPENDIX II

THE CHEMISTRY OF THE TOMB

By A. Lucas, O.B.E., F.I.C.

THE present note is a continuation of that bearing the same title that formed Appendix II of the second volume of " The Tomb of Tut·ankh·Amen."

As the clearance of the tomb progressed, not only were fresh materials of chemical interest brought to light, but also additional examples of materials of which specimens had already been found. These may now be described, as also certain of those that, although discovered during the earlier stages of the work, were previously either not referred to at all or were only given a very brief mention, as it appeared probable that similar materials might be present in greater quantity in the chambers then still to be cleared. This has proved to be the case, and these may now appropriately be more fully dealt with.

In the previous volume the fact that fungus growths occur in the tomb was briefly recorded. In the Antechamber there is a slight distribution of brown fungus spots, looking like rust, on the walls; in the Burial Chamber the walls are completely covered with a network of fungus, resulting in considerable defacement of the painted scenes; in the Innermost Treasury there is a slight amount of fungus, though more than in the Antechamber, and there is still more in the Annexe. No instance of fungus on the walls of other tombs in Egypt can be traced. The fungus, too, was not confined to the walls of the tomb, but occurred on many of the objects, being most marked on those that were either painted or covered with gesso and gold; the reason for this, as also for the large amount on the walls of the Burial Chamber (which alone is painted), being almost certainly that the glue used as a binder in the paint and in the gesso and that employed to fix the gold to the gesso provided an excellent nutrient medium on which the fungus could grow.

Not only, however, did the distribution of fungus vary on different kinds of objects, but sometimes it varied also on different parts of the same object. Thus, all the boats in the Innermost Treasury are painted, the colours generally being white, brownish-yellow, blue, green, red, black and canary-yellow. In every instance there was a large amount of fungus on the white, brownish-yellow, blue and green, but very little on the red and black, both of which colours, however, are present in comparatively small proportion, and as a rule none on the canary-yellow, or, at the most, a very small amount. The fungus, which was reddish, was often so thick that the original colour of the paint was entirely obscured. This was particularly noticeable on the blue pigment, the excessive growth on which is attributed to the fact that this pigment, being of a coarse granular nature, required a greater amount of adhesive to act as a binder (and therefore of food material for the fungus) than was the case with the other colours. The practical immunity of the canary-yellow, which consists of orpiment (sulphide of arsenic), was probably due to this pigment being poisonous to the fungus.

The remarkable pink coloration that was mentioned in the previous volume as occurring in the Antechamber, is also present in the other three chambers, being most marked in the Annexe; it is not confined to the walls, but is found also on the floors and ceilings. A pink coloration in tombs is not unknown in Egypt and occurs for instance on the plaster in the tomb of Imhotep at Lisht, excavated by the Metropolitan Museum of Art, New York. A similar coloration may also be seen on some ancient mortar recently uncovered near the sphinx at Giza and doubtless elsewhere. It seems probable that this coloration, which is merely superficial, has been caused by moisture dissolving some ferrous compound present in the stone and plaster, which was then brought to the surface by capillary attraction and there oxidized to ferric oxide (which may be almost any shade of red), but why the colour should be pink on the limestone and plaster and scarlet on the calcite veins in the stone is not clear.

The materials to be described will be taken in alphabetical order, as was done in the previous volume, those already fully dealt with or not having any special chemical interest being omitted.

Insects. As stated in the previous volume, specimens of the various dead insects found in the tomb were submitted for identification to Mr. A. Alfieri (then entomologist at the Royal Agricultural Society, Cairo, and now in the Ministry of Agriculture). It was stated that these insects were small beetles, such as feed upon dead organic matter and that they were all of kinds common in Egypt at the present day,

3,280 years not having made any modification in their size or structure, but the names of the beetles were not given and this may now be done.

1. From the Alabaster Vase No. 16 :
   Lasioderma serricorne, Fabr.
   Sitodrepa panicea, L.
2. From Alabaster Vase No. 58 :
   Lasioderma serricorne, Fabr.
3. From Alabaster Vase No. 60 :
   Lasioderma serricorne, Fabr.
   Gibbium psyllioides, Czemp.
4. From Alabaster Vase No. 61 :
   Lasioderma serricorne, Fabr.
5. From Box No. 115 :
   Lasioderma serricorne, Fabr.
   Sitodrepa panicea, L.
   Gibbium psyllioides, Czemp.

All the above-named insects are beetles, *L. serricorne* and *S. panicea*, belonging to the family of the *Anobiiœ*, and *G. psyllioides* to that of the *Ptinidœ*.

Metals. The metals were of the same kinds as those previously found, except that there was not any lead, which, however, was only present before in the shape of one very small piece. The various colours on the gold from the first two chambers have already been described and all these, including the very characteristic rose colour, were also present on the gold from the Innermost Treasury and Annexe. In the case of several objects, however, particularly one walking-stick, the gold is covered with a thin red coating that proved on analysis to consist of coloured glue. The amount of material available for examination was too small for the nature of the pigment to be determined, but it is probably of mineral origin.

The silver and electrum found in the Innermost Treasury and Annexe exemplified a new feature, namely, that the tarnish, instead of consisting of a thin film of silver chloride, as was the case with the silver and electrum from the Antechamber and Burial Chamber, was often a thicker coating of silver sulphide. The cause of the difference needs explanation, and it seems probable that the sulphur required to form the sulphide was derived from the orpiment employed as a pigment on various boats and other objects, since no other source of sulphur was apparent. This explanation, if accepted, would mean one of two things, namely, either that some of the orpiment became disintegrated into fine powder and was disseminated about the rooms, or that it became chemically decomposed and that the sulphur, or more probably sulphuretted hydrogen formed from it, was diffused through the air and coming into contact with the silver and electrum, acted upon them, forming a coating of silver sulphide. Although the former hypothesis is not impossible, the latter appears the more probable, and it is suggested that some of the orpiment was decomposed by means of fungus, with the formation of sulphuretted hydrogen, since it is well known that certain kinds of fungus do decompose sulphur compounds and produce sulphuretted hydrogen. The only difficulty about the acceptance of this explanation is that the orpiment was the one pigment on which there was practically no fungus, but the difficulty may be overcome by assuming that where the orpiment was contiguous to another pigment on which there was fungus, as was frequently the case, some slight action may have taken place along the edges of the orpiment. That the sulphur required to form the sulphide of silver did originate in the orpiment is confirmed by the occurrence of a thick coating of sulphide, and practically no other form of corrosion, on certain miniature copper tools that were packed in the same box as some *Shawabti*-figures on which there was orpiment, whereas other tools from boxes containing similar figures, but without orpiment, were free from sulphide, the corrosion consisting of carbonate and oxychloride. It should be noted, too, that in those instances in which silver objects were protected from contact with orpiment or the products of its decomposition, as, for example, the silver handles of the sledge on which the Canopic Chest rested (which was covered with a shrine), the silver was free from sulphide. These handles, too, exemplify another feature that may be mentioned, namely, that irregularly-distributed yellowish patches occur in the silver, which are manifestly due to the presence of gold, a phenomenon not uncommon in ancient Egyptian silver.

Many of the objects that are either of copper or bronze have not yet been analysed, but where analysis has been possible, as with some of the miniature tools accompanying the *Shawabti*-figures, the metal was found to be copper, generally entirely free from tin or containing only a trace. In a few instances, however, tin was present in small amount, but in no specimen tested was it in greater proportion than about two per cent., and such material may reasonably be regarded as impure copper rather than as bronze. This does not mean, however, that there was not any bronze in the tomb, since some of the objects that it has not been possible to examine chemically are almost certainly bronze. In this connexion may be mentioned a material that proved to be oxide of tin. This consisted of a number of thin fragments (from 1 mm. to 6 mm. in thickness) that apparently originally had all been one piece; the material was fairly brittle, dark-grey in colour and showed a crystalline fibrous structure at the broken edges. Several of the fragments were very slightly curved, suggesting that they had possibly been plastic and had formed a layer at the bottom of a curved vessel. The whole appearance was that of a secondary and not a primary material, and until it was analysed it was thought to be possibly a partially-exhausted ore. The specific gravity and hardness as determined by Mr. O. H. Little of the Geological Survey of Egypt were 5·0 to 5·4 and 6 respectively, and when examined by the Chemical Department, Cairo, the material was found to be oxide of tin. As it had not the appearance of a natural cassiterite it was subsequently submitted to Mr. R. H. Greaves, Controller of the Department of Mines, Cairo, who kindly sent it to Mr. W. G. Wagner, of Messrs. G. T. Holloway and Co., the well-known metallurgists of London, who was good enough to make a quantitative analysis, which showed that it had the following composition :

		Per cent.
Tin oxide	. . . .	94·80
Moisture	. . . .	1·23
Combined water	. . . . . .	3·97
Organic matter	. . . . . .	trace
		100·00

Mr. Wagner stated that the material was probably an artificially-prepared tin oxide.

Whether this was made in Egypt or not there is no evidence to show, but it seems possible that it was for use in the manufacture of opaque white glass, which is known to have been made in the Eighteenth Dynasty by the use of tin oxide.

The iron present in the Innermost Treasury and Annexe was limited to the blades of sixteen miniature tools that have already been described by Dr. Howard Carter, and it need only be mentioned that the total weight of the iron is only about four grams. The exact weight could not be determined without removing the blades from the handles, which was not desirable, and it could only be estimated from the weights of three of the blades that were loose and these weighed 0·20, 0·20 and 0·25 gram respectively. The blades, although very small and thin, were in fairly good condition and still consist largely of metallic iron with only a slight coating of oxide on the surface.

Minerals. Small lots of various mineral substances were found in the Annexe, which on analysis proved to be respectively chalk, galena, malachite (a few fragments of which had previously been found on the floor of the Antechamber), red ochre, yellow ochre, orpiment and two small irregular lumps of quartz sand, the grains of which were cemented together in one case by oxide of iron and in the other by a mixture of oxide of iron and oxide of manganese, and both of frequent occurrence as veins in the Nubian sandstone. All these substances occur naturally and, with the exception of orpiment, they are all found native in Egypt. The use of these materials, except the ferruginous sand, as pigments is well-known in ancient Egypt, galena and malachite having been employed for painting round the eyes, and malachite, chalk, red ochre, yellow ochre and orpiment for painting walls, furniture and various other objects, and this latter use is well exemplified in the present tomb. Both the red and yellow ochre had probably been prepared for use by separating the finer particles of the raw material from the coarser by lixiviation with water and then pressing the fine powder into a lump while wet.

Natron. Natron, or natural soda, consists essentially of carbonate and bicarbonate of soda, but as found in Egypt, it practically always contains common salt and sodium sulphate (sulphate of soda) as impurities. Natron occurs in several localities in Egypt, particularly in the Wâdî Natron in the western desert, but also in the north of the Behera province at Harrara and near El Kab in Upper Egypt. Natron was employed in Egypt in connexion with mummification certainly as early as the end of the Third Dynasty.

In the present tomb four different lots of natron occurred, namely, one in a small vase in a black varnished kiosk in the Burial Chamber, a second in a small vase at the entrance to the Innermost Treasury, where it was mixed with a gum-resin, and the third and fourth also in the same chamber in vases placed in front of the Canopic canopy. In each case the material was in the form of a fine crystalline powder, white or light-brown in colour; it was analysed qualitatively and identified by the writer and subsequently was submitted by him to Dr. H. C. Cox, F.I.C., London, for a quantitative analysis, which was impossible at Luxor. The results of Dr. Cox's analyses, which have been re-arranged, were as follows :

	BURIAL CHAMBER.	INNERMOST TREASURY.		
		A	B	C
	Per cent.	Per cent.	Per cent.	Per cent.
Natron (sodium carbonate and bicarbonate) . .	94·0	35·7	84·7	73·8
Common salt .	0·5	39·5	1·5	13·0
Sodium sulphate .	5·5	24·8	13·8	13·2
	100·0	100·0	100·0	100·0

There was no evidence of natron on the mummy, a few small whitish spots on the skin proving to be common salt containing a little sodium sulphate.

Pigments. Various minerals found in the tomb that were commonly employed as pigments have already been described. Two of these same substances, namely chalk and red ochre, also occurred prepared ready for use in shells, as also a greenish pigment, which was probably artificial frit (of which one small piece had been found previously on the floor of the Antechamber), but which could not be examined chemically without disfiguring the specimen, and a black powder, probably carbon, of which only traces remained. Enclosed in the remains of a linen bag was a granular blue powder which, on examination, proved to be the artificial frit so characteristic of ancient Egypt, which consists of crystalline copper-lime-silicate and of which several small pieces had previously been found on the floor of the Antechamber.

The pigments on a number of objects were also examined chemically. It will readily be realized that, although analyses of all the pigments from the tomb would be of value, yet it is only when fragments had fallen off that any examination could be carried out. The pigments tested from objects in the Innermost

Treasury and Annexe were the blue, canary-yellow and white from some of the boats, the white from a chair and two stools, the blue from some *Shawabti*-figures and from a box and the brown from a box.   In every instance the blue was artificial frit ; the canary-yellow was orpiment (sulphide of arsenic), probably obtained from Persia or Asia Minor, since, so far as is known, it does not occur native in Egypt, where there is no evidence of its use until the Eighteenth Dynasty ; the white was calcium carbonate (whiting), and the brown was a mixture of oxide of iron and calcium sulphate, possibly prepared artificially by adding finely powdered gypsum to red ochre in order to obtain the desired shade of colour.

Although the other pigments were not available for chemical analysis, it is fairly certain, judging by appearances, that the red is red ochre, the brownish-yellow is yellow ochre, and the black is carbon, probably some form of soot.   The green on the boats, however, is not green frit, such as was found on several objects from the Antechamber and of which a small piece was also found, but is possibly powdered malachite, an ore of copper that occurs in the country and that was employed as a pigment from a very early period.

Other pigments analysed were from three palettes. Two of these palettes hold two colours only, namely black and red.   The black is carbon and the red is red ochre in both cases.   The third palette at one time had six colours, but only five (black, red, green, white and yellow) remain, one (probably blue) being missing.   The black and red are carbon and red ochre respectively ; the green was not available for examination ; the white is probably calcium sulphate, but the quantity available was not sufficient for this to be confirmed ; the yellow is orpiment.

Resin. This material was very plentiful in the tomb, and its occurrence in the Antechamber and Burial Chamber has already been dealt with. It was present also in the Innermost Treasury and Annexe, both as a true resin and as a gum-resin, the former being in the natural condition as lumps ; as worked objects (large beads, ear studs, etc.) ; as black varnish and as an adhesive ; and the latter in the form of small tears and rods, mixed with natron. The lumps are reddish-brown and translucent and without any easily-recognizable characteristic whereby they might be identified ; the resin of the beads and other objects is very dark red by transmitted light, but black by reflected light, and this also has not yet been identified. The black varnish has previously been described. The gum-resin is in the form of very small tears and rods, the latter 2 to 5 mm. long and 0·5 mm. in diameter, white on the outside from adhering natron and from their own fine dust, but yellowish-brown in the interior : it has not yet been identified, but it is certainly not myrrh and it has not the appearance of frankincense. In this connexion the incense mentioned in the previous volume may be further described. The amount of material available for examination was so small that only a few preliminary tests were possible. The substance is of a yellowish-brown colour, brittle, slightly resinous-looking, burns with a smoky flame, giving off a pleasant aromatic odour, and when tested it was found to have a solubility of approximately 80 per cent. in alcohol and 20 per cent. in water after alcohol, and is therefore a gum-resin and so cannot be ladanum, Mecca balsam or storax, and from the colour it is probably not myrrh, bdellium or galbanum ; altogether it is suggestive of frankincense that has been powdered and made into balls artificially.

Stones. The stones employed for jewellery and inlay found in the Innermost Treasury and Annexe were largely repetitions of those already described. The principal were carnelian, of which there was a considerable quantity ; lapis lazuli, of which in the aggregate there was also a large amount ; quartz, generally translucent and employed with a red cement to imitate carnelian ; calcite, also translucent and often set in red cement like the quartz, but sometimes yellowish and used without the red cement ; green felspar ; turquoise, usually greenish, though occasionally a good sky-blue colour ; one specimen of amethyst ; one example of yellow chalcedony, two previous specimens having been colourless and green [1] respectively ; red jasper ; one example of green and one of brown serpentine as inlay ; a little black steatite as inlay ; flint ; obsidian for eyes and pupils of eyes ; crystalline limestone for the whites of eyes, and a hard, dark olive-green stone used for a large scarab, which has not been identified. Another stone also not yet identified, of which there were several examples from the Burial Chamber and one from the Antechamber, is a hard, opaque stone with a slight greenish tint, not unlike callais or faded turquoise matrix in appearance.

The stones, other than those employed for jewellery and inlay, included alabaster (calcite) for vases,

[1] This, which is a signet ring, has since been further examined. Its specific gravity is 3·4 ; it is not marked by a steel point or by quartz, but will not scratch glass and is therefore not chalcedony nor nephrite (jade), but probably jaedite.

Shawabti-figures and the Canopic box; flint for miniature tools; dark grey speckled granite for *Shawabti*-figures; crystalline limestone for bracelets and anklets; quartzite for *Shawabti*-figures; dark serpentine for a vase; black steatite for imitation black pigment on several palettes; slate for palettes and a hard, grey, quartzose stone for hones.

Sugar. The residue from one of the many alabaster jars in the tomb consisted of a dark resinous-looking matrix in which were embedded small, light-brown coloured particles, the surface of the whole being covered with innumerable, tiny, dead beetles. The lighter coloured particles were crystalline and proved on analysis to be sugar. The nature of the matrix has not yet been determined, but it is not sugar, resin or gum. The identity of the original material, therefore, remains uncertain, but it does not appear to have been honey, which was the principal sweetening matter employed in ancient times, and it is suggested that it may have been a fruit juice, such as grape juice, that has dried and largely decomposed and from which the sugar has crystallized out.

Wine. The solid matter from the bottom of a pottery jar that, both from its shape and from an inscription on it, is undoubtedly a wine-jar, was found on analysis to be, as was only to be expected, impure " tartar " (argol) and therefore a wine residue, definite positive tests having been obtained for tartrate, potassium and carbonate. An interesting fact about the specimen was the large proportion of potassium carbonate present, which suggests a decomposition of part of the original tartrate.

APPENDIX III

Plates

PLATE I

A PORTRAIT HEAD OF TUT·ANKH·AMEN

A carved wood and painted portrait head of the young boy king, represented, traditionally, springing from a lotus flower, like the young Sun-god who sprang from the primeval waters. It was discovered in the Entrance Passage of the tomb.

PLATE II

ANUBIS GUARDING THE ENTRANCE OF THE INNERMOST TREASURY

(*See* pp, 33, 41, Plate VI)

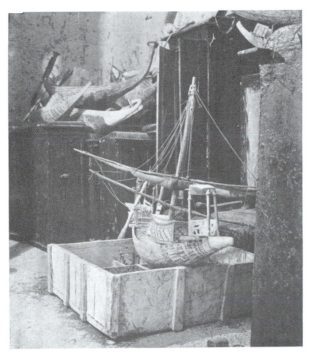

A

B

Plate III

INTERIOR OF THE INNERMOST TREASURY: SOUTH SIDE

(*See* pp. 33, 51)

A

B

PLATE IV

INTERIOR OF THE INNERMOST TREASURY: NORTH SIDE

(See pp. 33, 34)

PLATE V

INTERIOR OF THE INNERMOST TREASURY: EAST END: THE
CANOPIC CANOPY

(See pp. 35, 47)

PLATE VI

THE GOD ANUBIS UPON HIS GILDED PYLON

(*See* pp. 33, 41, Plate II)

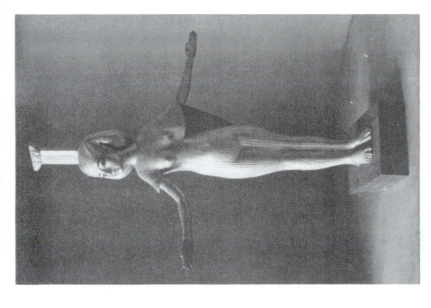

ISIS

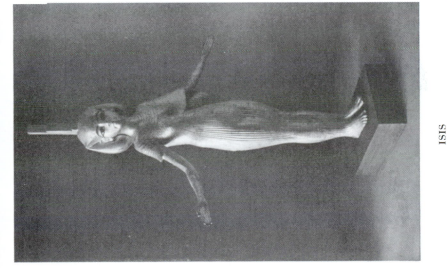

NEPHTHYS

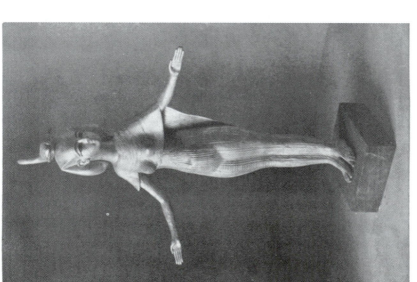

NEITH

SELKIT

(*See* Plate V)

PLATE VIII

THE TUTELARY GODDESSES FROM THE CANOPIC CANOPY

A

B

Plate IX

THE ALABASTER CANOPIC CHEST

(A) The pall covering the chest.   (B) The chest

PLATE X

THE CANOPIC CHEST OPEN

Showing the four human-headed lids, sculptured in the likeness of the king, that
covered the four receptacles for the viscera.

(*See* Plate LIII, B)

PLATE XI

STATUETTES OF DIVINITIES : HOUSED IN BLACK WOODEN
SHRINE-SHAPED CHESTS

(*See* p. 51, Plate LVI, B.C.)

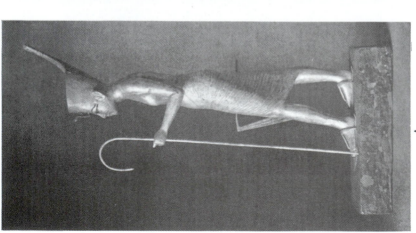

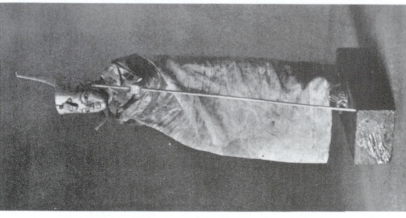

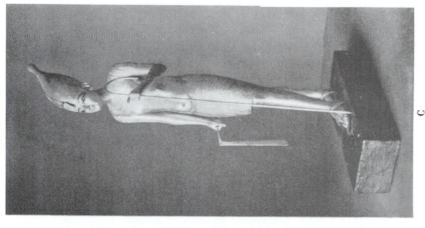

PLATE XII

STATUETTES OF THE KING

(A and B) wear the crown of Lower Egypt; and (C) the crown of Upper Egypt.

(*See* p. 54)

PLATE XIII

STATUETTE OF THE KING

Representing Tut.ankh.Amen as the Youthful Warrior Horus killing the Typhonial
Animal.

(*See* p. 55, Plate LX)

PLATE XIV

STATUETTE OF THE KING UPON A BLACK LEOPARD

(*See* p. 56)

A

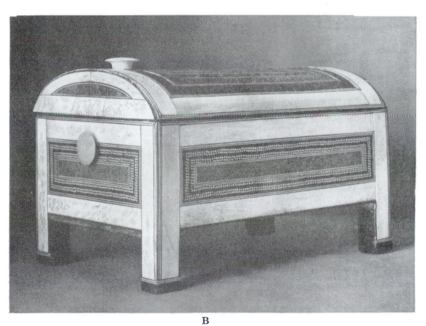

B

Plate XV

TWO TREASURE CASKETS ORNAMENTED WITH IVORY AND
EBONY MARQUETRY

(*See* p. 66, Plate IV)

A

B

PLATE XVI

AN OVAL CASKET WITH LID IN THE FORM OF THE KING'S CARTOUCHE

(*See* p, 67, Plate IV)

A

B

PLATE XVII

(A) THE KING'S OSTRICH-FEATHER FAN
(B) A CASKET OF CEDAR WOOD, IVORY, GOLD, AND SILVER

(*See* p. 67, **Plate IV**)

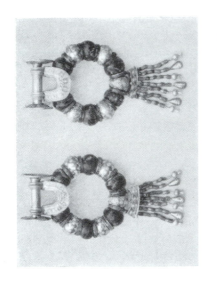

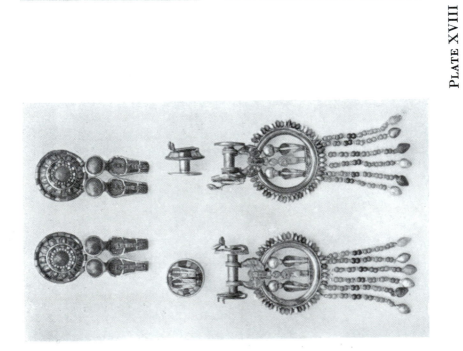

(See p. 74)

PLATE XVIII

THE KING'S EAR-RINGS

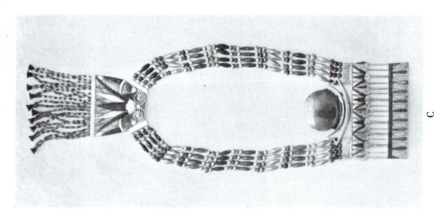

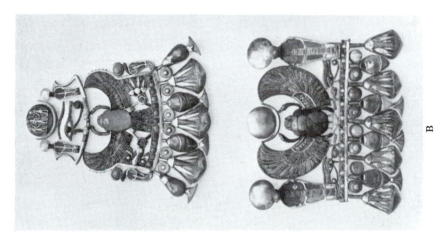

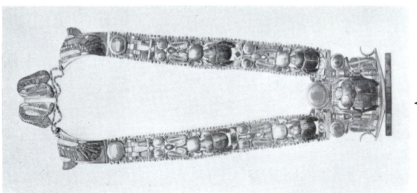

A

B

C

PLATE XIX

PECTORAL ORNAMENTS

(*See* p. 76)

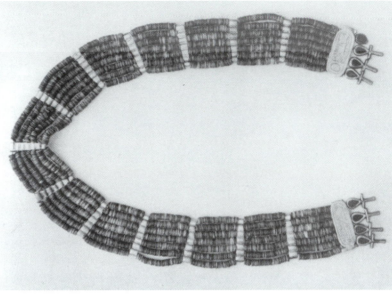

B

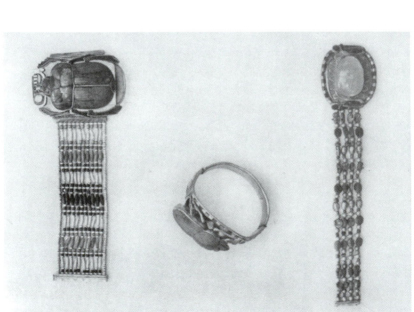

A

PLATE XX

(A) BRACELETS. (B) A BEAD AND GOLD CEREMONIAL SCARF

(See pp. 77, 79)

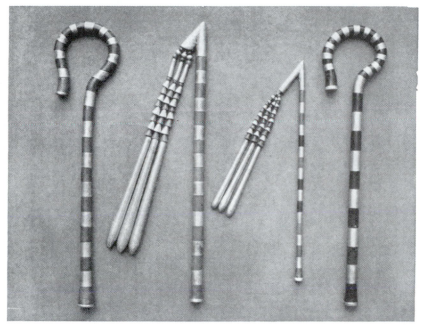

A

B

PLATE XXI

(A) THE KING'S SCEPTRES
(B) TWO MIRROR CASES

(See pp. 77, 78)

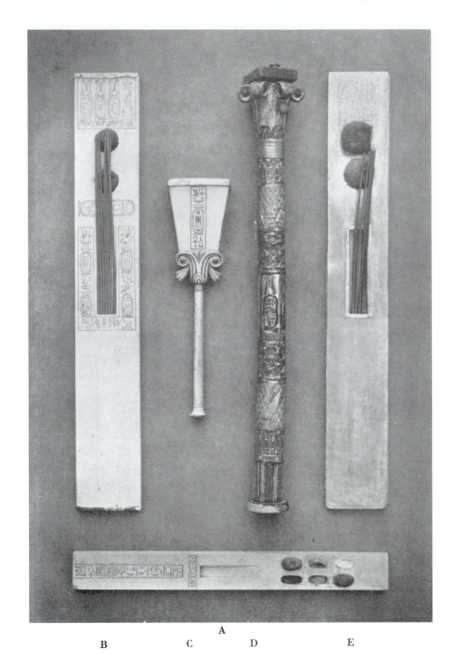

A

B   C   D   E

PLATE XXII

THE WRITING OUTFIT

(A) Ivory palette of Mert·Aten   (C) Ivory burnisher of the king

(B) Ivory palette of the king   ˙(D) Reed case of the king

(E) Gold palette of the king

(*See* p. 79, Plate LXVI)

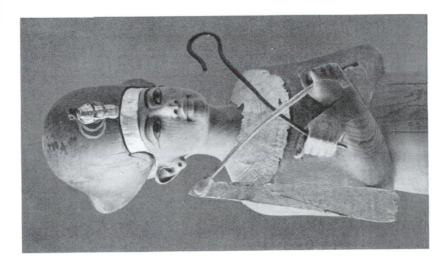

(*See* p. 82, Plate LXVII)

PLATE XXIII

A *SHAWABTI*-FIGURE OF THE KING

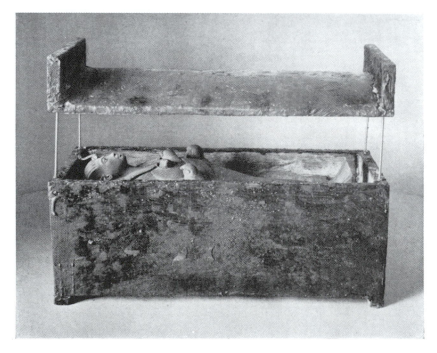

PLATE XXIV

AN EFFIGY OF THE DEAD KING

(*See* p. 84)

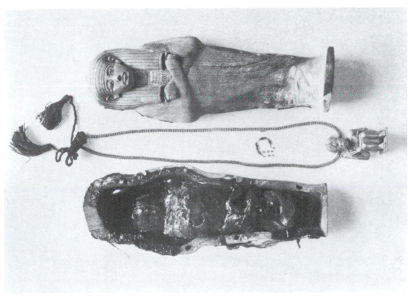

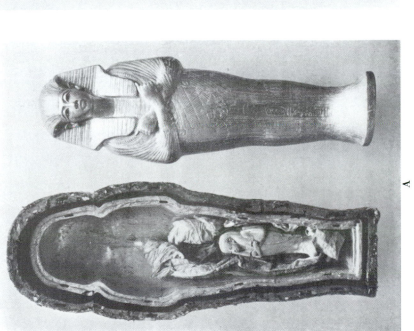

PLATE XXV

HEIRLOOMS

(A) A miniature set of two coffins. (B) A third smaller coffin. (C) A gold chain and statuette of Amen-heltep III; and (D) a fourth minute coffin containing a lock of Queen Tyi's hair.

(*See* p. 86)

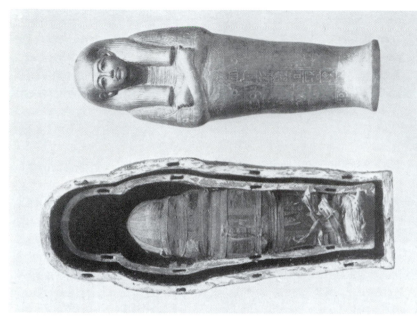

A

B

PLATE XXVI

THE COFFINS AND MUMMIES OF TWO STILL-BORN CHILDREN

(See p. 88, Plate LI)

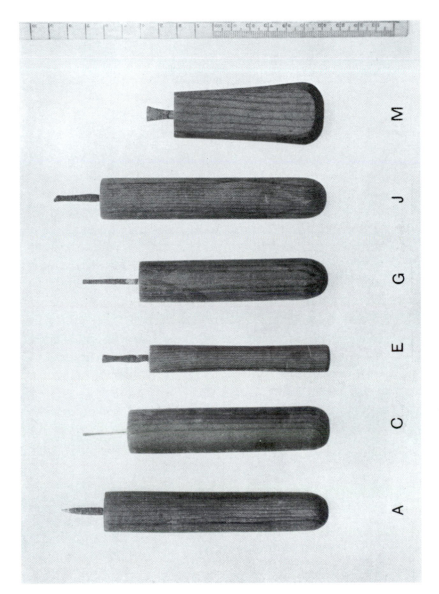

A   C   E   G   J   M

PLATE XXVII
A SET OF IRON IMPLEMENTS

(See p. 89)

A

B

Plate XXVIII

(A) THE KING'S BOW-CASE
(B) DETAILS OF THE CENTRAL PANEL

(*See* p. 94, Plate XXIX)

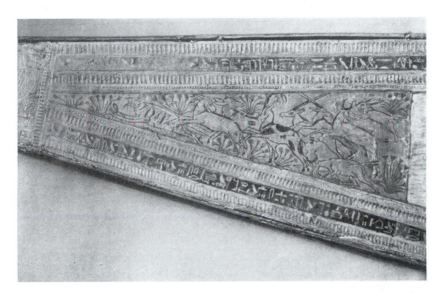

A

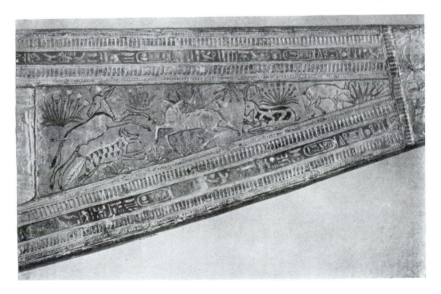

B

PLATE XXIX

THE KING'S BOW-CASE
(A) Details of left, and (B) right hand panels.

(*See* Plate XXVIII)

A

B

Plate XXX

INTERIOR OF THE ANNEXE AS SEEN FROM THE DOORWAY
Note the footprints of the dynastic robbers upon the white bow-box (B).

(*See* Plate XXXI)

PLATE XXXI

THE ANNEXE IN PROCESS OF BEING CLEARED

(*See* Plate XXX)

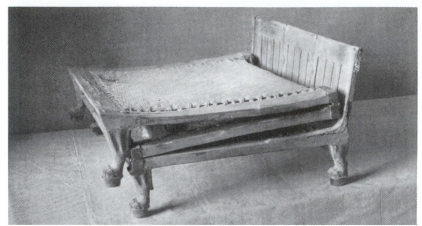

A

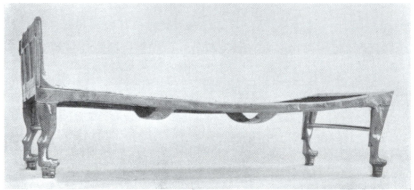

B

C

Plate XXXII

(A) A FOLDING CAMP BEDSTEAD
(B) A GOLD-PLATED BEDSTEAD
(C) DETAILS OF FOOT-PANEL OF GOLD-PLATED BEDSTEAD

(*See* p. 110)

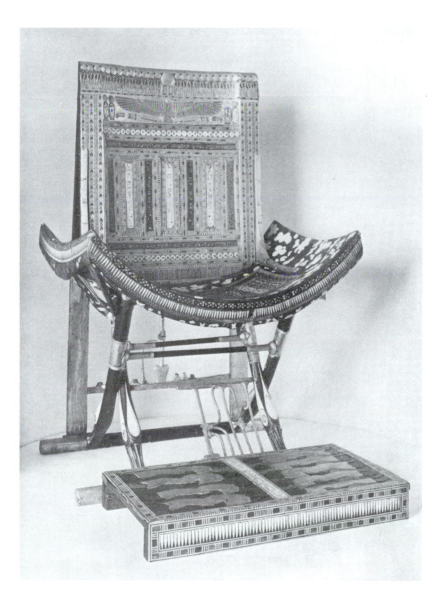

PLATE XXXIII

THE KING'S ECCLESIASTICAL THRONE AND FOOTSTOOL

(*See* p. 111)

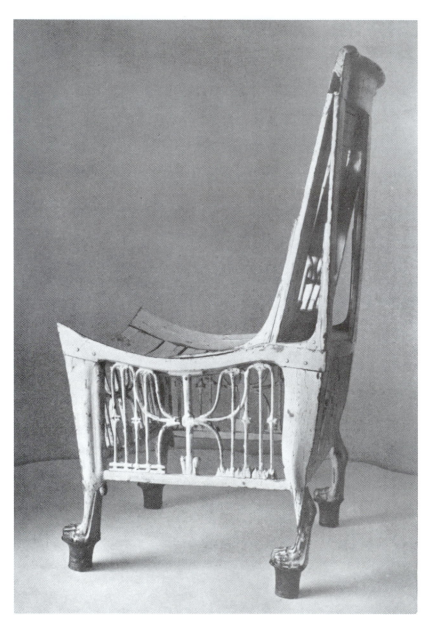

PLATE XXXIV

A WHITE WOODEN CHAIR

(*See* p. 113, Plate LXVIII)

B

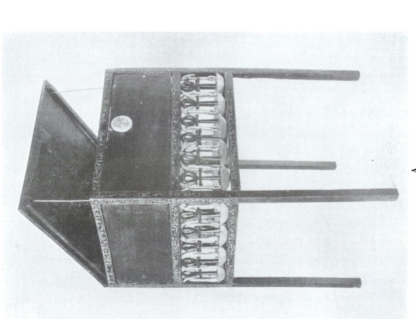

A

Plate XXXV

TWO TABLE-SHAPED CABINETS

(*See* p. 115, Plate XXX)

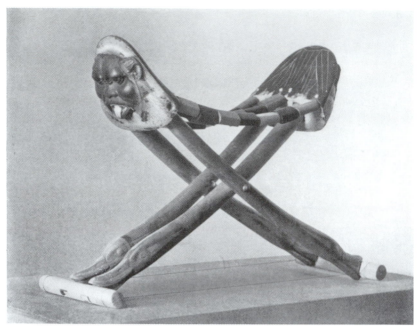

A

B

Plate XXXVI

TWO HEAD-RESTS CARVED OF IVORY

(*See* p. 116, Plate LXX)

A

B

PLATE XXXXVII

A BOX FOR THE KING'S HEAD-WEAR

(*See* p. 119)

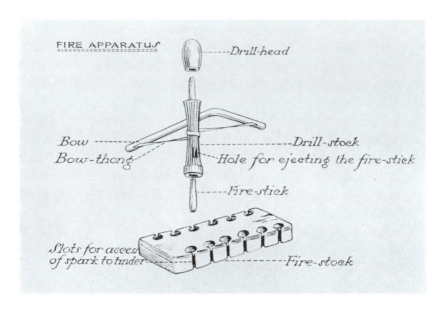

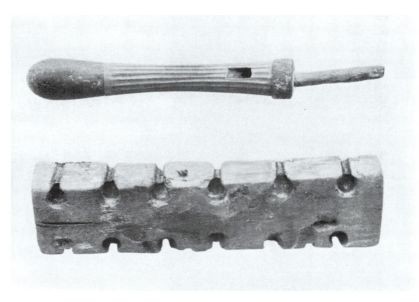

PLATE XXXVIII

A FIRE-MAKING APPARATUS

(*See* p. 121)

Plate XXXIX

A LINEN DALMATIC DECORATED WITH TAPESTRY-WOVEN AND
NEEDLEWORK ORNAMENT

(See p. 124)

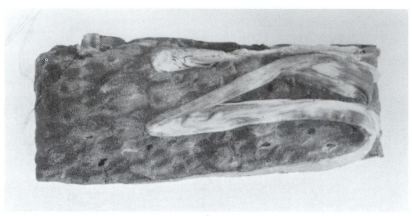

A

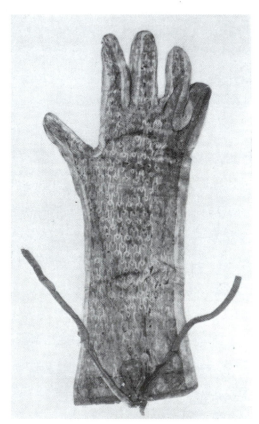

B

PLATE XL

A PAIR OF TAPESTRY-WOVEN LINEN GLOVES

(A) A glove as discovered, neatly folded.
(B) The fellow glove after unfolding.

(See p. 126)

PLATE XLI

AN ALABASTER ORNAMENTAL CENTRE-PIECE IN THE FORM
OF A BOAT FLOATING IN A TANK

(*See* p. 127, Plate **LXXIV**)

B

(*See* p 130, Plate LXXV

PLATE XLII

THREE IVORY GAMING-BOARDS AND PLAYING-PIECES

PLATE XLIII

THREE OSTRICH-FEATHER FAN-STOCKS

Fan-stock (A) of embossed gold; (B) of carved and stained ivory; and (C) of ebony veneered with decorative backs. (D) Showing the quills of the ostrich feathers still *in situ*.

(*See* p. 132)

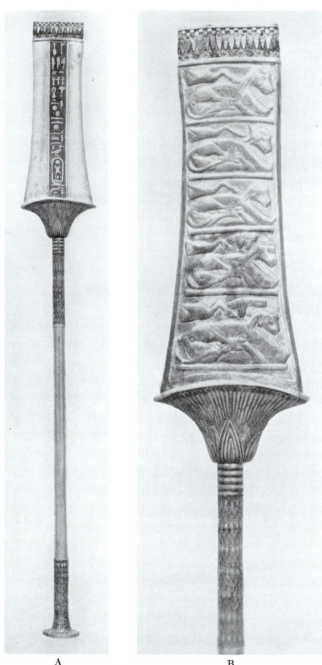

A   B

PLATE XLIV

THE KING'S *KHERP*-SCEPTRE

(*See* p. 133)

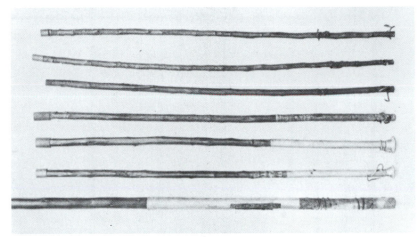

A

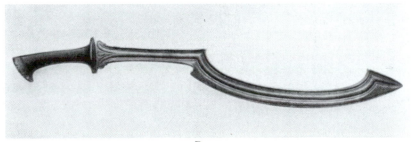

B

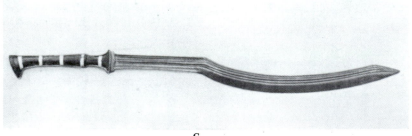

C

Plate XLV

ARMS OF OFFENCE

(A) Single-sticks.   (B and C) Two bronze falchions

(*See* p. 136)

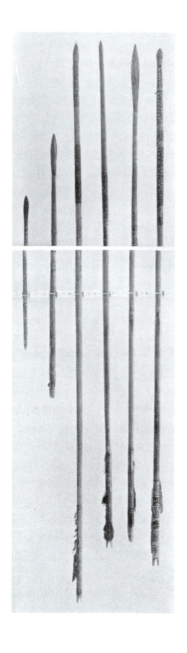
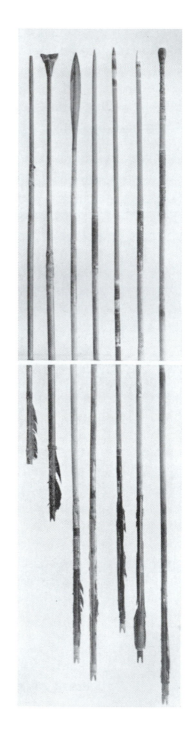

(*See* p. 139)

PLATE XLVI

ARMS OF OFFENCE: ARROWS OF DIFFERENT TYPES AND SIZES

A

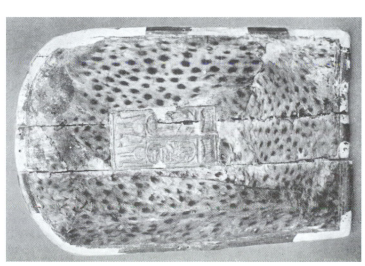

B

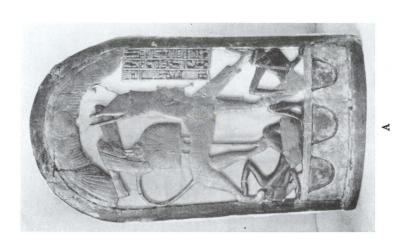

C

Plate XLVII

ARMS OF DEFENCE

(A and C) Ceremonial shields of heraldic design. (B) Shield of hard wood lined with cheetah skin.

(*See* p. 142)

PLATE XLVIII

AN ALABASTER UNGUENT VASE IN THE FORM OF A MYTHICAL LION

(See p. 146)

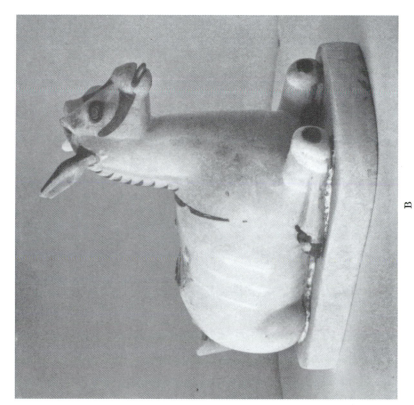

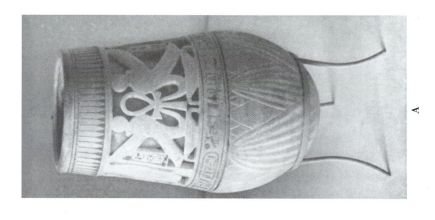

A

B

PLATE XLIX

(A) AN ALABASTER CRATER FOR OIL. (B) AN ALABASTER IBEX VESSEL FOR OIL

(*See* p. 147)

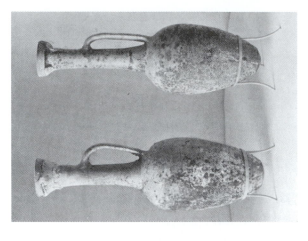

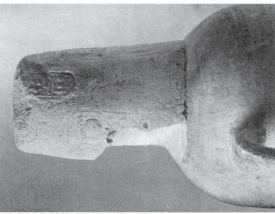

C

B

A

PLATE L

WINE-JARS

(A) Wine-jars with dockets and seals intact.　(B) The capsule showing subsequent smaller seal.　(C) Wine-jars of foreign form.

(*See* p. 147)

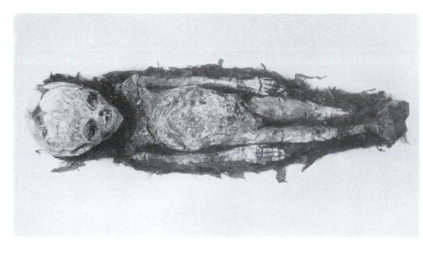

B

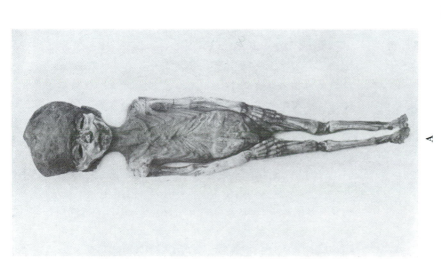

A

Plate LI

THE TWO HUMAN FŒTUSES DISCOVERED IN THE TOMB

(*See* p. 88, Plate XXVI)

A

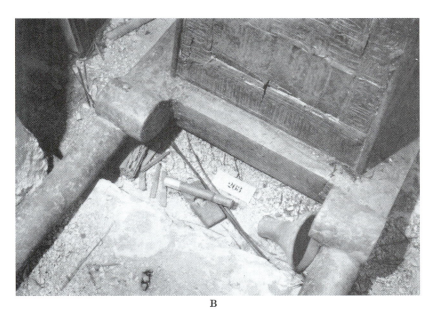

B

PLATE LII

PLATE LII

THE MAGICAL FLAME

(A) A small reed torch mounted with gold-foil and stood upon a clay-brick pedestal with magical formula scratched upon it.

(B) The torch and pedestal as it was found within the threshold of the Innermost Treasury, in front of the Anubis pylon.

(*See* pp. 33, 40)

PLATE LIII

DETAILS OF THE CANOPIC CHEST

(A) One of the four seals that secured the lid of the Canopic chest.

(B) The interior of the Canopic chest showing the counterfeit rectangular compartments and rims of jars. Within each counterfeit jar will be seen the head of the gold coffin (Plate LIV) for the viscera.

(*See* pp. 35, 46, Plates IX, X, LIV)

A

B

PLATE LIII

PLATE LIV

PLATE LIV

A MINIATURE GOLD COFFIN FROM
THE CANOPIC CHEST

One of the four miniature gold coffins that contained the viscera of the king. They are similar in
design to the second coffin that enclosed the king's
mummy, but they are far more elaborately inlaid in
feather-design, and each coffin bears the formula
pertaining to the goddess and her genius under whose
charge it was placed.

(*See* pp. 35, 46, Plates IX, X, LIII)

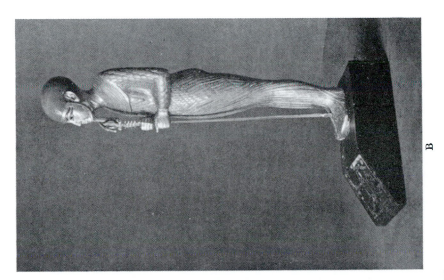

PLATE LV

A

B

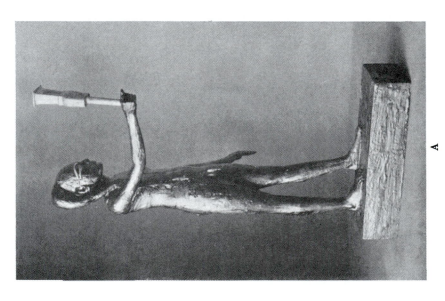

A

B

C

PLATE LVI

Plate LVI

STATUETTES OF DIVINITIES

(A) An *Ihy*-musician, carved of wood and coated with black resin.

(B) Imsety, the genius of Isis.

(C) A divinity named Mamu.

The latter two divinities (B and C) are of wood plated with gold, and Plate XI depicts them, as discovered, within their shrine-shaped chests.

(*See* pp. 52 ff.)

Plate LVII

A GOLD-PLATED STATUETTE OF THE DIVINITY MENKARET

This remarkable group represents the deceased king, being held upon the head of the divinity Menkaret. The exact purpose is not known, but possibly so that the dead king may see the glorious luminary, the sun.

(*See* pp. 52 ff.)

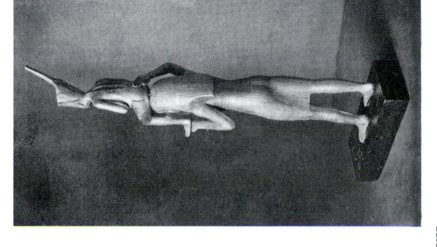

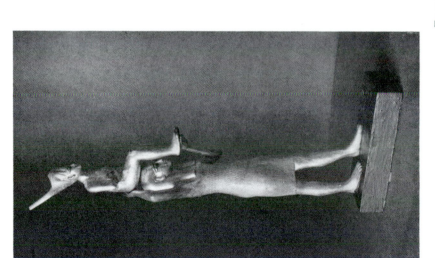

Plate LVII

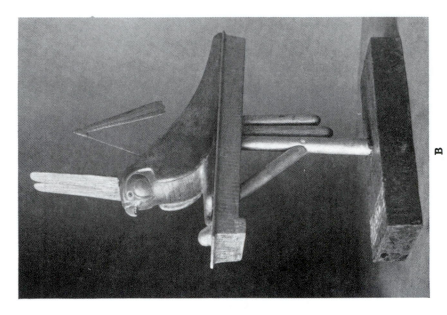

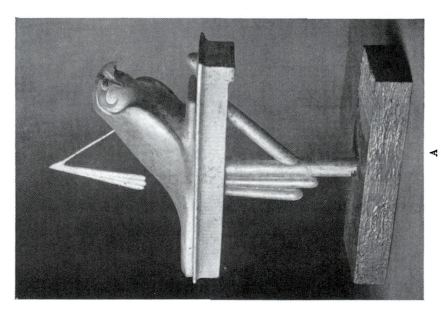

A   PLATE LVIII   B

PLATE LVIII

TWO GOLD-PLATED FALCON STANDARDS

(A) A falcon standard named Gemehsu.

(B) A falcon standard named Spedu.

These may possibly be two forms of the Falcon Standard of the ancient XXth Nome of Lower Egypt, like the two standards, found in the Antechamber, of the Xth Upper Egyptian Nome (Vol. I, p. 114).

(*See* pp. 52 ff.)

Plate LIX

EMBLEMS OF THE WORLD BEYOND THE GRAVE

(A) The golden head of the Meh·urit cow.

(B) A serpent divinity named Neter·ankh.

(*See* pp. 33, 46, 53)

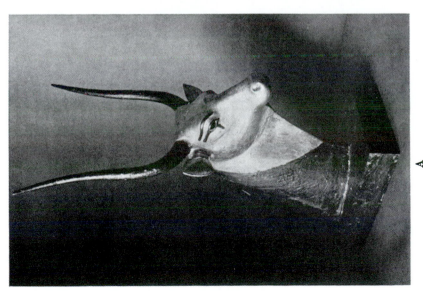

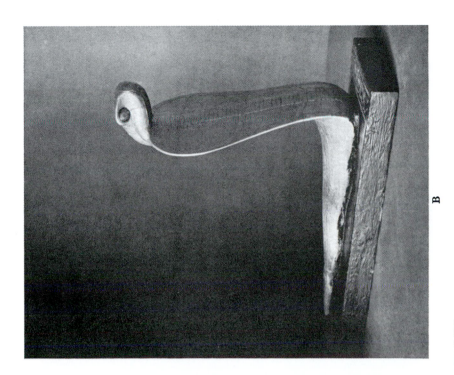

B

A

PLATE LIX

PLATE LX

PLATE LX

A STATUETTE OF TUT·ANKH·AMEN

A wooden gold-plated statuette representing the king as the Youthful Warrior Horus upon a reed-float in the act of killing the Typhonial Animal. It is probably the ancient Egyptian prototype of St. George and the Dragon of the Christian Era. It is one of a pair of statuettes found in a black shrine-shaped chest and was carefully draped in linen.

(*See* pp. 54 ff., Plate XIII)

PLATE LXI

CELESTIAL CRAFT

(A) One of the four ships to follow the divine journeys of the sun. Amidships is the gilded throne for the royal passenger.

(B) One of the two canoes for ferrying across to the fields of the blessed.

(*See* pp. 56 ff.)

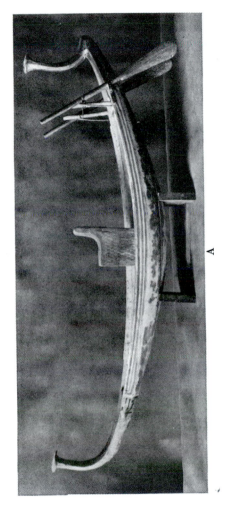

A

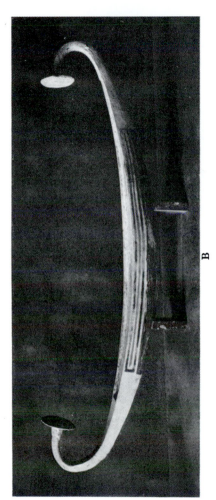

B

PLATE LXI

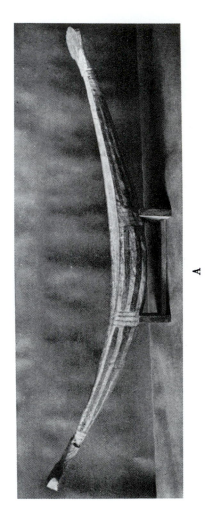

A

B

PLATE LXII

PLATE LXII

A CANOE OF PRIMITIVE TYPE

(A) A model reed-float, or canoe, for the mythical pastimes of Horus—the King.

(B) A survival of this primitive reed-float still in use in the upper reaches of the Nile.

(*See* pp. 59 ff.)

TWO CRAFT FOR THE FUNERAL PILGRIMAGE

(A) A model of a fully rigged ship, with cabin amidships and gilded pavilion on the forecastle and poop decks, that towed the funeral barges (B) belonging to the funeral pilgrimage. Upon the forecastle and poop of the barges are small "look outs," and amidships a large double-roofed cabin.

(*See* pp. 60 ff.)

A

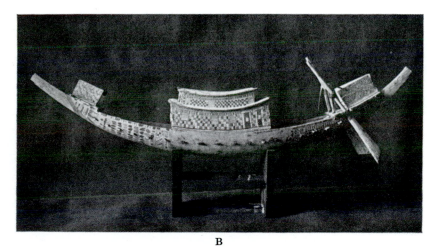

B

PLATE LXIII

A

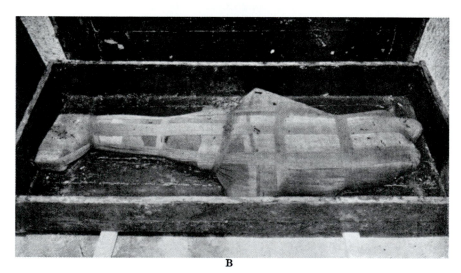

B

PLATE LXIV

PLATE LXIV

A GERMINATED EFFIGY OF OSIRIS

(A) A wooden frame moulded in the form of Osiris, hollowed out, filled with silt, and planted with corn.

(B) The effigy, as discovered in a box, completely wrapped in linen winding-sheets.

(*See* p. 61)

PLATE LXV

(A) A model strainer of wood and copper for brewing beer.

(B) A model " thrusting " hand-mill for grinding corn.

(C) A model granary, showing doorway and separate compartments for storing cereals.

(*See* pp. 61, 62, 63)

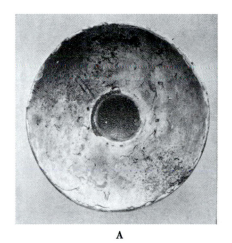

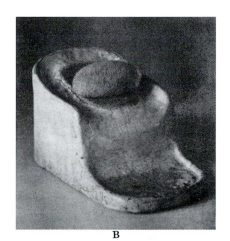

A

B

C

PLATE LXV

A

B

PLATE LXVI

PLATE LXVI

PART OF THE KING'S WRITING OUTFIT

(A) An ivory bowl stained red, and (B) a papyrus basket belonging to the King's writing outfit. The basket has highly coloured pictures upon it depicting the King before Amen-Re, Herakhte, Ptah, and Sekhmet.

(*See* pp. 79 ff., Plate XXII)

PLATE LXVII

AGRICULTURAL IMPLEMENTS AND KIOSKS FOR THE *SHAWABTI*-FIGURES

(A) Model hoes, picks, yokes, baskets, and water vessels, in blue faience, for the use of the *Shawabti*-figures.

(B) Small wooden kiosks, covered with black resin, in which the figures were housed.

(*See* pp. 81 ff., Plate XXIII)

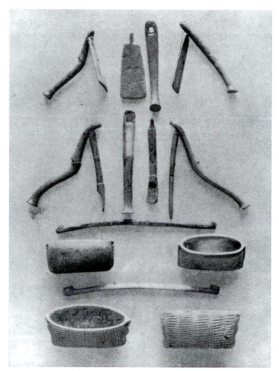

A

B

PLATE LXVII

A

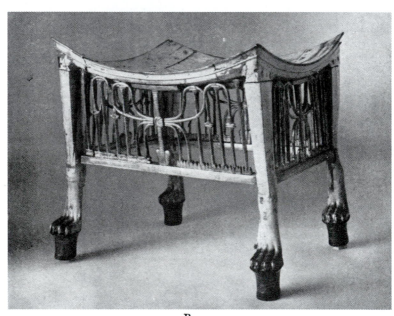

B

PLATE LXVIII

PLATE LXVIII

A PAIR OF STOOLS

(A) A three-legged semi-circular stool of wood, painted white.

(B) A four-legged wooden stool painted white, with gilded traditional ornament between the seat and stretchers.

(*See* p. 114, Plate XXXIV)

PLATE LXIX

A FOOTSTOOL AND HASSOCK

(A) A small footstool made of cedar wood, and inlaid with ivory and ebony.

(B) A hassock of rush-work, lined with linen, and covered with elaborate polychrome beadwork depicting alien captives bound and prone round a central rosette.

(*See* p. 115)

A

B

PLATE LXIX

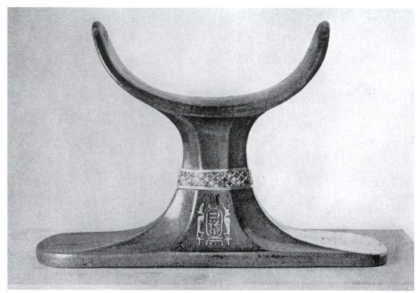

A

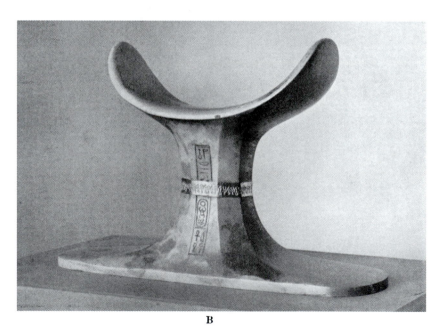

B

PLATE LXX

PLATE LXX

A PAIR OF HEAD-RESTS

(A) A head-rest of lapis lazuli blue faience mounted
with inlaid gold collar.

(B) A head-rest of turquoise blue glass mounted
with an embossed gold collar.

(*See* pp. 116 ff., Plate XXXVI)

PLATE LXXI

CHESTS BELONGING TO THE KING'S
EARLY YOUTH

(A) Two small chests of pannier type, made of cedar wood, ebony and ivory.

(B) A chest for the knick-knacks and playthings of Tut·ankh·Amen's youth.

(*See* pp. 119 ff.)

A

B

PLATE LXXI

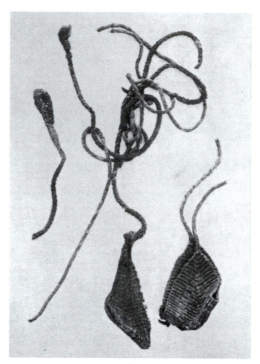

A

B

PLATE LXXII

Plate LXXII

(A) The remains of two plaited linen-thread slings for hurling stones.

(B) Cakes prepared in palm-leaf shapes.

(*See* pp. 122 ff.)

Plate LXXIII

SILVER AND FAIENCE VESSELS

(A) A silver vase in the form of a pomegranate fruit.

(B) Pale and dark blue faience vases.

(C) Pale blue faience libation vessels.

(*See* pp. 123 ff., 130)

A

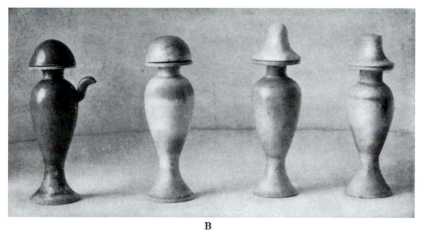

B

C

PLATE LXXIII

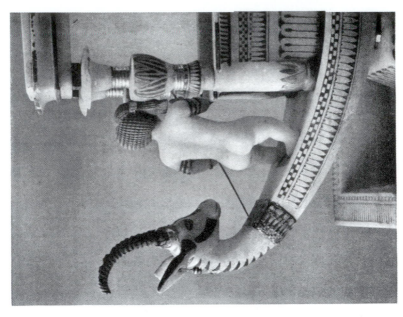

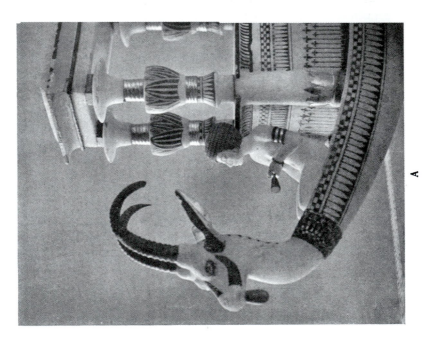

PLATE LXXIV

A

B

PLATE LXXIV

DETAILS FROM THE ORNAMENTAL ALABASTER BOAT

(A) The figure of a nude girl squatting and holding a lotus flower on the fore-deck of the boat.

(B) The female figure of an achondroplasic dwarf at the helm, steering the boat.

The head-dresses of both the figures are made of a dark green stone.

(*See* pp. 127 ff., Plate XLI)

PLATE LXXV

A GAMING-BOARD AND "THROWING-STICKS"

(A) A set of four "throwing-sticks" having backs of ebony and underpart of ivory, which, by the manner of their fall, denote the moves upon the gaming-board.

(B) A reversible gaming-board of ebony and ivory having on the top a game of three by ten squares, and on the bottom a game of three by four with an approach of eight squares.

(*See* pp. 130 ff., Plate XLII)

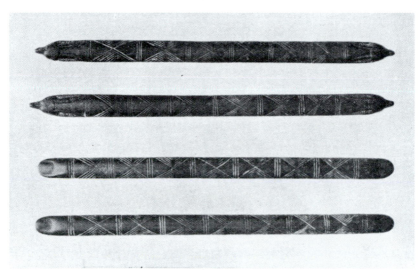

A

B

PLATE LXXV

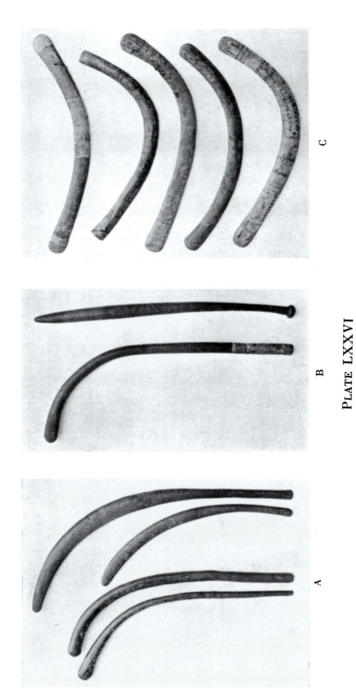

PLATE LXXVI

A

B

C

PLATE LXXVI

WEAPONS OF OFFENCE

(A) Falciform clubs of hard wood, with either the suggestion of a knob at the end, or with flattened blade cut like a sickle.

(B) A falciform club with bark handle, and a cudgel-shaped club. Both are of hard wood.

(C) Boomerangs of hard wood and painted.

(*See* pp. 135 ff., Plate LXXVII)

Plate LXXVII

WEAPONS OF OFFENCE

Figs. A and B depict various types of the boomerangs and throwing-sticks of hard wood decorated with bark.

(*See* pp. 135 ff., Plate LXXVI)

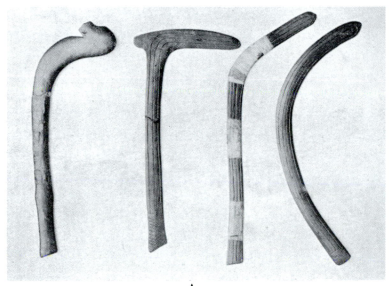

A

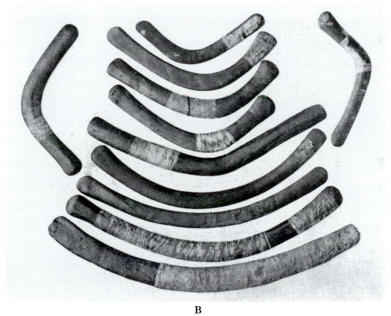

B

PLATE LXXVII

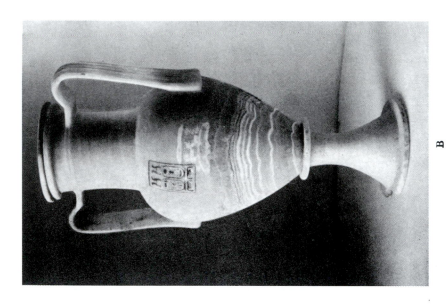

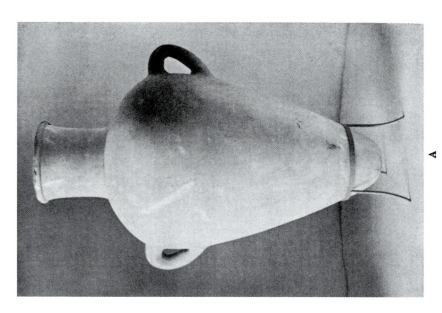

PLATE LXXVIII

PLATE LXXVIII

ALABASTER VESSELS FOR OIL

Figs. A and B depict two of the larger oil-jars found in the Annexe.

(*See* pp. 144 ff., Plates XLVIII, XLIX, LXXIX)

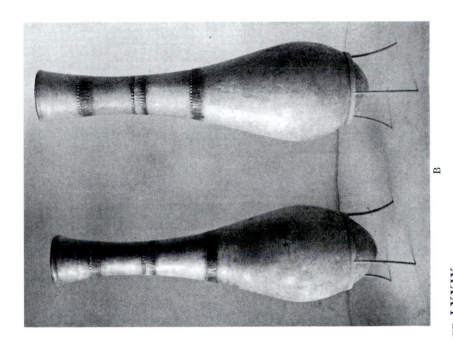

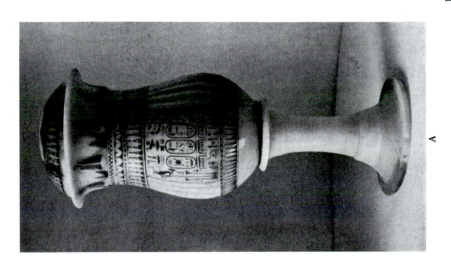

A

B

PLATE LXXIX

A

B

C

D

PLATE LXXX

PLATE LXXX

FRUIT BASKETS

Figs. A, B, C, and D illustrate the characteristic types among the 116 fruit baskets discovered in the Annexe.

(*See* pp. 149 ff.)

INDEX

A

ADZE of bronze and gold, 134

Akh·en·Aten, ascended throne, 3 ; co-regency with Amen·hetep III, 3 et seq. ; assumed new name, 14 et seq. ; mother of, 6 ; reign of, 6 et seq. ; wives of, 11, 23 ; daughters of, 12 et seq. ; regnal years of, viii, 11 et seq. ; age of, 10 et seq., 14 ; cache of, 10 ; mummy of, 10 ; alabaster vessel of, 146 ; fan of, 133

Akh·et·Aten, the city of, 8 et seq.

Alfieri, Mr. A., 172

Almina, Countess of Carnarvon, vi et seq.

Amen, return to the cult of, 17, 23, 26 et seq.

Amen·hetep III, reign of, 2 et seq. ; dated monuments of, 3 et seq. ; co-regency with Akh·en·Aten, 3 et seq. ; birth and coronation of, 7 ; robbed of his nomen, 9 ; death of, 16 ; gold statuette of, 87 ; alabaster vessels of, 146

Amen·hetep IV, see Akh·en·Aten

Amulets, 143

Ankh·es·en·Amen, 6, 13, 27 ; marriage of, 21, 148 ; issue of, 27, 88

Ankh·es·en·pa·Aten, see Ankh·es·en·Amen

Ankh·khepru·Re Mery·nefer·khepru·Re, see Smenkh·ka·Re

Anklets, 121, 123

Annexe, v, 98 et seq., 144

Anubis, 33, 41 et seq. ; symbols of, 41 ; jewellery of, 42, 74

Arrows, 27, 138, 139 et seq.

Aten, 7 et seq. ; Domain of, viii, 147 ; names and titulary of, 15

Atum, the sun-god, 52

Auta, the sculptor, 6

Ay, 25 ; as regent, 27 ; as king, 26 ; and Tut·ankh·Amen, 26 ; with Ankh·es·en·Amen, 28 ; length of reign, 28 et seq.

B

BABES, still-born, 27 et seq., 88, 167 et seq.

Bakt·Aten, Princess, 5 et seq.

Baskets of fruits, 98, 104, 105, 149 et seq.

Bedsteads, 104, 110 et seq.

Benretmut, sister of Nefer·titi, 25

Bes, the household god, 117

Boat of alabaster, 102, 127 et seq.

Boats, see Craft

Boomerangs, 127, 141 et seq.

Bow-box, 127

Bow-case, 34, 94 et seq.

Bows, 95, 138 et seq.

Box of Smenkh·ka·Re, 17 et seq.

Boxes, 33 et seq. ; 64 et seq. ; 86, 89, 98, 99, 118 et seq. ; stolen contents of, 69 ; for head-wear, 119 et seq.

Bracelets, 77, 121, 123

Bracers, archers', 121

Breasted, Professor James H., 28, 100

Burial equipment, 35 et seq.

Burnisher for papyrus paper, 81

Burton, Mr. Harry, vi, ix

C

CABINETS, table-shaped, 102, 115 et seq.

Canopic-equipment, 34 et seq., 46 et seq.

Carnarvon Estate, vi

Cases, wooden oviform, 104

Caskets, see Boxes

Chairs, 111 et seq.

Chariots, 34, 38, 96

Chests, shrine-like, 33, 51 et seq. ; for travelling, 119 ; see also Boxes

Chicago, Expedition of the University of, 28

Children of Tut·Ankh·Amen, 27, 88, 167 et seq.

Climatic conditions in Egypt during dynastic times, 153 et seq.

Clubs, wooden, 127, 135 et seq.

Coffins, miniature, 86 et seq. ; of children, 88 ; for viscera, 47, 49

Collars, bead, 76

Cost of the work, vi et seq.

Cow, the Meh·urit, 33, 46

Cox, Dr. H. C., 178

Craft, model, 33, 39, 56 et seq., 143

297

Index

Index

Index